ADULT LEARNIN
AND SOCIAL DIVISIⴑN
– A PERSISTENT PATTERN

A report of the findings of a UK-wide survey on
adult participation in education and learning
carried out for NIACE
by Research Surveys of Great Britain (RSGB)

NAOMI SARGANT and
FIONA ALDRIDGE

niace

promoting adult learning

Published by the National Institute of
Adult Continuing Education (England and Wales)

21 De Montfort Street
Leicester LE1 7GE
Company registration no. 2603322
Charity registration no. 1002775

First published 2002

NIACE has a broad remit to promote lifelong learning
opportunities for adults. NIACE works to develop
increased participation in education and training,
particularly for those who do not have easy access
because of barriers of class, gender, age, race, language
and culture, learning difficulties and disabilities, or insufficient
financial resources.

NIACE's website is www.niace.org.uk

Cataloguing in Publication Data
A CIP record of this title is available from the British Library.

Designed and typeset by Boldface
Printed in Great Britain by Alden Press

ISBN: 1 86201 155 9

Contents

List of tables and figures

Tables

Figures

Introduction

Naomi Sargant has led NIACE's work mapping adults' participation in formal and informal learning for 20 years now, and the Institute can trace its surveys back to the 1920s. It is a mark of the effectiveness of this work and the complementary programme of qualitative studies on barriers to participation and how they might be overcome, that the issue of who is not 'there' is so clearly on the policy agenda.

Since the last survey in 1999, the Learning and Skills Act has put in place the national Learning and Skills Council (LSC) together with 47 local Learning and Skills Councils bringing new information needs. Devolution also requires new research approaches.

The Government established a National Adult Learning Survey (NALS) in the mid-1990s, and has now adopted the English Local Labour Force Survey (ELLFS) to secure a large annual snapshot and also provide data for individual LSCs. A national target for adult participation in learning was adopted in 1998, and the Learning and Skills Council will set its own target in 2003. A range of other participation studies have appeared: enriching debate, understanding and dialogue about mechanisms to secure a learning society in which everyone feels able and confident to participate.

This year our publication is in two parts. In the first, Naomi and Fiona Aldridge report on the detailed findings of the 2002 survey, and how those findings relate to trends over time. In the second, a range of other voices explore the linkages between NIACE's work and the Department for Education and Skills' series on the findings for Wales, Scotland and Northern Ireland and on the wider social debate about the relevance, focus and accuracy of such studies. They are produced to encourage reflection, discussion and argument.

When the welcome decision was taken to regularise the adult participation dimension of the English Local Labour Force Survey, NIACE considered whether there was a case for continuing the sequence. On balance we decided that there was. The NIACE survey, unlike others, is easily replicable for local area studies, at relatively low cost. Its findings have a stable relationship with NALS/ELLFS findings – and the gap between the two usefully captures the difference between overall participation and people's perception of themselves as learners and potential learners. This gap represents a major challenge to providers seeking to widen and deepen participation.

There are, of course, omissions here. Our sampling method, like the ELLFS one, fails to do justice to the complexity and diversity of participation by Britain's diverse ethnic and linguistic communities. A major discrete parallel study is needed to address that gap. There is, too, a need for longitudinal studies: with luck the National Adult Learning Survey will develop into a learning-focused longitudinal study.

Meanwhile, I am grateful to Naomi Sargant and Fiona Aldridge for writing and editing the book, to John Kruk and his colleagues at RSGB for their unfailing help and efficiency in carrying out their work, to each of the essayists for their contributions, and to the European Social Fund for financial support. The message of the study overall is uncompromising – we have a long way to go to narrow, let alone close, the divide in the United Kingdom that separates the learning-rich and the learning-poor.

Alan Tuckett
Director
NIACE

Key findings

Introduction

1.   *Adult learning and social division: a persistent pattern* reports on a survey carried out for NIACE, the National Institute of Adult Continuing Education, by Research Surveys of Great Britain (RSGB). A sample of 4,896 adults aged 17 and over across the four UK nations was interviewed between 13 February and 3 March 2002.

2.   The national sample for Wales was boosted to 1,000, four times its correct proportion, in order to enable a separate report for Wales to be produced, but the samples for each nation are shown in their correct proportions in this report. Copies of the full set of analyses for both the UK and Wales are available on request from NIACE.

Stability of the 2002, 1999 and 1996 surveys

3.   The survey shows a high degree of stability with both the 1996 and 1999 surveys, and confirms that the UK still faces an enormous task in involving all its people in the learning society, and that the learning divide between the learning-rich and the learning-poor continues to exist.

Leisure and lifestyle

4.   Participation in learning is, for adults, a matter of choice and has to be fitted in with work, family and other interests and obligations. The use of leisure is affected by opportunity, and social changes are combining with technological changes to expand some opportunities while others are being contracted or even closed down. Increasingly some people are learning in the workplace, whether for work or personal reasons. For some people the boundaries between work and leisure are virtually invisible.

5.   People still spend more time watching television (over 3-and-a-half hours per day) than they do on any other activity except sleeping and working (if they are in work). Men have more leisure time than women and this gap is widening as more women enter the labour-market but still have to cope with the double agenda of work and family.

Main leisure activities and interests

6.   The proportions recording social activities as their main leisure interest have remained stable across the 20 years at 44% to 46%. Reading dominated the list in 1980 (48%) and 1990 (51%) but has dropped by 10% to 41%, yet is still the most important activity among women (51%) in 2002.

7.   Sports and physical activities showed a big increase between 1980 and 1990 and now appear stable. They now have equal ranking with reading at 41%, though men engage in sports much more than women (49% compared with 35%).

8.   In 1980 and 1990, all the domestic arts and skills such as DIY, handicrafts, cookery and needlework etc were grouped together. These are now separated showing the gender differences more clearly but recording an overall drop of 5% in such activities.

9.   Some leisure interests are related to age, family position and location. Not surprisingly, social and sports activities figure more highly among the young, while gardening and sewing/knitting increase gradually with age. There is a serious drop (10%) in the proportion mentioning voluntary or committee work and its incidence is appreciably higher among the four older age-groups. The proportion naming gardening has also dropped, by 6% and its incidence is much higher among those older age-groups. More armchair gardeners do not necessarily lead to more gardening.

10.   Reading maintains a significant proportion across all the age-groups. Separated out for the first time as leisure activities are the creative arts, which rank at 10% or more across all the age-groups except those aged 75 and over. Also included for the first time as a main leisure activity is going to church or mosque *etc* – an activity which increases with age.

Leisure interests and activities, socio-economic class and type of area

11.   Virtually every activity is engaged in by proportionately more of the higher socio-economic classes than the lower ones. The only exceptions to this are reading and sewing/knitting *etc* which increase slightly among DEs (unskilled workers and people on limited incomes), a group which includes more older women. It is surprising to find fewer C2s (skilled manual workers) and even C1s (white-collar workers) engaging in social activities and sport.

12.   While it is less surprising to find more of the higher classes engaging in the creative arts and in voluntary service, the descending graph for church-going is less obvious.

13.   Urban dwellers read more and engage more in social activities while rural dwellers garden more and engage more in sport and physical activities.

Ethnicity and leisure activities

14.   The 'black' group ranks sport and physical activities highest at 47%, followed by reading (41%) and social activities (35%). The Asian group, the largest studied, places social activities highest (45%), followed by reading (42%), then sporting and physical activities (32%). The 'other ethnic' category also places social activities highest (48%), followed by reading (41%) and sports (36%). The next highest activities for all three groups are gardening, DIY/handicrafts and creative arts. Of all the groups, the Asian group places 'place of worship' the highest at 9%.

Relationship of leisure activities to learning

15.   Current learners engage at a higher rate in social activities (56%), sports and physical activities (55%), reading (47%) and creative arts (19%) and indeed in most of the smaller categories of activities. The activities which do not vary much across learning status are reading, gardening and DIY/handicrafts, with sewing/knitting etc increasing marginally among non-learners. Many other activities reduce among less active learners or non-learners. Activity seems to breed activity.

The use of cultural and community facilities

16.   The 1990 survey recorded a drop from 1980 in the regular use of libraries of 5%. This drop appears to have stopped and libraries are visited at least once a month by over 30% of all age-groups, with the proportion rising to over 40% among those aged 17-24. It is encouraging that many libraries are extending their role in relation to learning and ICT facilities with the People's Network.

17.   Twenty-two per cent of black and 21% of Asian people visit public libraries at least once a week, twice the proportion in the general population. However, they are used by 10% more ABs and C1s than C2s and DEs.

18.   Cinema-going has increased dramatically from 15% going at least once a month in 1990 to 32% in 2002. There is a small increase in those going once a week from 1% to 4% and a doubling of people going from once a week to once a month, from 14% to 29%. Cinema-going is mainly an activity of the young with 72% of the youngest age-groups going at least once a month, but the proportions drop dramatically with increasing age. C1s are the class that goes to the cinema most (40% each month) but even one in five (22%) of the DEs go at least once a month.

19.   Theatre-going has increased since 1990, from 6% to 10% going at least once a month, with 2% more women than men. Visits to the theatre and to concerts/opera/ballet are heavily skewed to the middle and upper classes and to the better-educated. The combination of concerts/opera/ballet is stable at 9% as is the proportion going to a museum at least once a month (9%), with art galleries lower at 6%.

20.   One in five go to a community centre/social club at least once a month (23%) and the proportion is the same for a place of worship (22%). Proportions attending both of these show a drop in the middle years, presumably reflecting other family ties. Religious attendance has remained stable over the two decades with 5-6% more women than men attending and the proportions rising with age. While there is little class difference in attending a social/community club, religious attendance is again heavily slanted to the middle and upper classes.

Relationship of cultural and community activities to learning

21.   Current learners engage in every single activity, whether specifically cultural or not, at higher rates than recent, past or non-learners. One half of current learners (51%) also visit public libraries once a month compared with 35% of the general population. Similarly, 51% of current learners go to the cinema once a month compared with 32% of the general population, and 28% of current learners attend a place of worship compared with 22% of the general population.

22.   More positively, 25% of those who have never learnt post-school do go to libraries at least once a month, as do 22% of the same group who go regularly to a community centre/club – also possible sites for learning.

23.   Recent, past and non-learners engage in all these activities at declining rates. The interlinkage of educational and cultural access and take-up is clear and reinforces the uneven distribution of social and cultural capital.

Current and recent participation in learning

24.   Nearly one in four adults (23%) are currently learning, with 42% of adults having participated in some learning activity during the last three years. Over one third of adults (36%) have not participated in any learning since leaving full-time education.

25.   The proportion of current/recent learners (42%) has increased by 2% since the 1996 and 1999 surveys, when 40% of adults said that they were current or recent learners.

26.   For the first time in 2002, men and women are currently participating in equal numbers (23%), although more women (39%) than men (34%) say that they have not done any learning since leaving full-time education.

27.   Socio-economic class remains a key determinant of adult participation in learning. Three-fifths of all upper- and middle-class respondents (AB) and 54% of C1s are current or recent learners, compared with 37% of C2s and only 25% of DEs.

28.   Adults in socio-economic groups AB are more than twice as likely to be current or recent learners as those in groups DE. Fifty-eight per cent of DEs have not participated in any learning since leaving school compared with just 17% of ABs.

29.   Since 1996, current participation has remained unchanged for all groups, except ABs, where small increases in participation were achieved in both 1999 and 2002.

30.   The workplace is not only a major location for learning, but also provides adults with information about learning opportunities, as well as the finance and motivation to take them up. Over one half of both full-time (52%) and part-time workers (51%) are current or recent learners, compared with 46% of the unemployed, 31% of those who are not working and just 19% of retired adults.

31.   Since the last major survey in 1999, the largest increase in learning has been among the unemployed, from 41% to 46%. Substantial increases in participation achieved between the 1996 and 1999 surveys, among part-time workers and those who are not employed have been further built upon and maintained respectively.

32.   The older people are, the less likely they are to participate in learning. Over 70% of those aged 17-24 are current or recent learners, compared with around a half of those aged 25-54. The decline in participation becomes particularly steep for those aged 55 and over, such that only 20% of adults aged 65-74 and 10% of those aged 75 and over are current or recent learners.

33.   Terminal age of initial education is a key predictor of participation of learning as an adult. The figures show a divide between those who leave school at the earliest opportunity and those who stay on, even for a short while. Only 30% of those who left school at 16 or earlier are current/recent learners. This compares with more than 45% of current/recent learners who stayed on at school post-16, and 65% of those who stayed on post-20.

34.   Participation across the nations and regions of the UK continue to display considerable differences that cannot be easily explained. Overall 42% of the UK population are current/recent learners. The national totals are Scotland, 44%, England, 42%, Northern Ireland, 40% and Wales 39%. Since 1999, participation has increased by 11 points in Scotland and 8 points in Northern Ireland, while it has fallen by 4 points in Wales.

35.   Highest participation levels within the English Government Office regions are reported in the South East (48%) and North East (46%). The North West (39%) and the Eastern region (36%) report the lowest levels of participation.

Future intentions to learn

36.   Forty-one per cent of adults say that they are very or fairly likely to take up learning in the next three years, a slight increase from the 1996 and 1999 figure of 38%.

37.   Fifty-seven per cent say that they are very or fairly unlikely to take up any learning in the future, 2% less than in 1999.

38.   For the first time, more women (41%) than men (40%) say that they are likely to take up learning in the future.

39.   Recent experience of learning continues to be a powerful influence on whether adults expect to learn in the future. Seventy-eight per cent of current learners report that they are likely to take up learning in the future, compared with only 13% of those who have not participated since leaving full-time education.

40.   Employment status also influences future intentions to learn. Only one in eight retired people see themselves as future learners, while around one half of those in employment say that they are likely to take up learning in the future. Unemployed adults (54%) see themselves as being most likely to take up learning in the next three years.

What people are learning about

41.   Apart from the continuing increase in computer studies, the pattern of subjects being studied shows a very similar picture to 1999 and 1996. The rate of increase in computer studies has slowed, with an increase of 4% between 1999 and 2002, compared with an increase of 8% between 1996 and 1999.

42.   The growth of computer studies comes at the expense of some other subject areas. Business studies has dropped by 4% since 1996, foreign languages by 3%, social sciences and social care by 3% and the general grouping of other professional and vocational qualifications from 18% to 12%. Given the impact of new communications technology and the increasing multi-disciplinary nature of many courses, some of these shifts are likely to be inter-related. Health studies, *etc*, has maintained its level at 10% in 2002. Creative arts with photography has also maintained its increase at 6% and has overtaken foreign languages which have continued to decline from their high point in 1990 and now record only 5%.

43.   Engineering and science/maths/statistics are stable at 4 or 5% and are studied more by younger groups, as are the social sciences, while foreign languages, creative arts and history are studied more by older groups.

Age differences in subjects studied

44.   The younger groups learn computer skills at lower rates than older people, presumably because many of them have already mastered the basics at school. All adult age-groups aged 25 and over are now learning computer skills at a higher rate than in 1999. Far more older people are studying computer skills: 36% of 55-64 year-olds; 28% of 65-74 year-olds; and 23% of those aged 75 and over.

45.   There is also evidence of returning to learning or up-skilling in the middle years (25-44) both in health/medicine (12%) and vocational and professional qualifications (17%).

Work status and subjects of study

46.   For many people, work provides both the incentive to learn and the place in which such learning may take place or be supported – for those in full-time work. Part-timers and the unemployed are less well-supported. Thirty-eight per cent of the unemployed and 33% of those who are not working are studying computer skills compared with 29% overall.

47.   Encouragingly, 12% of those working part-time and full-time are studying health/medical care. Ten per cent of the unemployed are studying engineering, and 11% are studying social sciences. Sixteen per cent of those working full-time and 12% of those working part-time are studying for professional or vocational qualifications.

48.   There are a number of small reductions in subjects which would have typically been provided through adult education and may have been a casualty of the Schedule 2 division of funding. It continues to be clear, and computer skills is the current example, that the same subject may fulfil a work-related purpose for some learners and a personal development purpose for others. It will be important to continue to offer a wide variety of subject choice as much of the provision wanted and needed by older people is likely to be different from that needed by the young.

49.   Considerably more women continue to give personal and educational reasons for their choice of study, while more men give work-related reasons, though the gap is narrowing.

50.   There is an increase in the proportion of people who choose their subject in order to gain a qualification or get on a course, from 11% in 1999, to 27% in 2002. However, it is likely that this is partly caused by respondents now being allowed to give more than one reason.

51.   The proportion aiming for a qualification from their course has gone up from 64% in 1999 to 66% in 2002.

52. Four per cent had no personal choice, the course was chosen by their employer and two per cent had to study it as a professional requirement.

53. The proportion of participants who are able to name subjects they would like to learn about in the future has dropped from 69% in 1996, to 66% in 1999, and 62% in 2002. This is not encouraging. Younger people up to the age of 44, current and recent learners, and ABs and C1s are more definite about their choices, while other groups are less so. There is a similar decline by social class, with 73% of ABs naming subjects, followed by 68% of C1s, 63% of C2s, and 51% of DEs.

54. Computer studies dominate the wish-list with 31% of men, 25% of women and 28% overall naming it as their preferred choice of course. The next highest subject is foreign languages (12%), followed by creative arts (7%), social sciences/social care (6%) history (6%), health studies/ medical care (5%), and then, all at 4%, a range of more traditional adult education subjects: handicrafts/DIY, gardening, flower-arranging, music, cookery, and business/management. Other subjects ranking at 3% or less cover a similar traditional variety: sports/keep-fit, engineering, accountancy, maths/science, driving, car maintenance, photography, needlecrafts and English.

55. Older people's wish-list, similarly, includes subjects which were in the past commonly provided by adult education institutions: foreign languages, creative arts, history/local history, gardening/floristry, DIY/carpentry, cookery and needlecrafts. Much of this conventional provision has been cut back and it will be necessary to reinstate it and offer it in accessible ways if older people are to be attracted back into learning.

Subjects of interest to current learners and to those likely to learn in the future

56. Current learners are interested in computer studies (15%), foreign languages (10%), creative arts (9%), other professional and vocational qualifications (5%), nursing/health studies (4%), business/management (3%), history/local history (3%) and other leisure subjects (3%).

57. Likely future learners show a similar pattern, but more of them are interested in computer studies (24%). There is a very wide range of other subjects which include foreign languages (9%), creative arts (9%), other professional and vocational qualifications (6%), nursing/health studies (5%), business/management (4%), history/local history (4%), music (4%), social sciences (4%), handicrafts/DIY (3%), cookery/catering (3%), engineering (3%), social work/care (3%), accountancy (3%), maths/science (3%), other academic subjects (3%), and 'other' leisure subjects (4%).

58. While these percentages appear small, it is important to remember that 1% of all likely future learners represents 200,000 adults.

Source of information about learning, its location and time spent on study

59.   Information advice and guidance become more important as people enter and re-enter learning opportunities throughout their lives. Different age-groups gain information about learning opportunities from different sources. Information technologies, both old and new, are expected to play an increasingly important role in the provision of information and advice, but the majority of sources are still local and personal.

60.   The workplace continues to dominate as the main source of information about learning for all age-groups from 25-64, with 20% reporting work/employer/training officer and 12% specifying work-mates. Friends and family are next at 13%, followed by further education (11%). Next, equally ranked at 7%, are newspapers/magazines, university/HE and school, followed by adult education centres/WEA, at 4%.

61.   More men than women (by 5%) quote their work or work-mates. More women quote family/friends, by 3%, or school, also by 3%, as a source.

62.   School (29%) and further education (27%) are important sources of information for 17-19 year-olds. Sources are more varied among 20-24 year-olds, 22% quoting university/HE, but 22% also quoting friends/family. School (20%) and further education (18%) continue to be important for 20-24-year-olds. The new Connexions (careers/guidance) Service is mentioned by only 5% of those age-groups.

63.   Adult education services are more important for middle-aged and older people, peaking at 8% among 55-64 year-olds. Also important for these age-groups are the informal sources such as friends/family, newspapers/magazines and printed publicity. Community centres/voluntary organisations are important for older people, with 5% of 65-74s and 8% of 75+ mentioning them. Libraries used to rank much higher, particularly among older people, but appear at 2%, to have lost their image as an information provider.

64.   Sources of information and advice vary across the nations of the UK. The workplace and workmates are the most important source of information in all four nations, though lowest in Wales. Further education ranks higher in Wales. University/HE rates lower in Scotland and Northern Ireland than in England and Wales. Northern Ireland prefers less formal routes such as friends/family, school or work-mates.

The information divide

65.   Despite all the hype, newer sources of information have still not yet reached most people, particularly older ones. The proportion mentioning the internet or the world wide web has increased but only by 1%, to 2%. Most people are still reliant on traditional sources of informa-

tion, mainly local and personal. The internet rates 1% overall, with 14 mentions of learndirect. More encouragingly, 4% of 20-24 year-olds mention the internet as their source of information, as do 4% of men compared with 1% of women. This benchmarking is valuable.

The location of learning

66.   Further education colleges continue to be the most reported location of learning at 21%, increasing 1% from 1999. Universities/HE (16%) have just overtaken the workplace (15%) as the next highest location, though much employer-supported learning will take place in other locations e.g. training centres. Further education colleges are still the main place of learning for 17-19 year-olds (49%), 20-24 year-olds (22%) and now also 25-34 year-olds (21%). Universities are the dominant location for 20-24 year-olds (50%).

67.   The proportion learning at home is effectively stable between 1996 and 2002 at 14-15%, though how they are learning is changing. In 1996 and 1999, 10% said they were learning informally from a book, with 5% learning from a structured open learning and 1% from TV/radio. In 2002, 6% are learning from a book, 6% from a computer, CD-Rom or the internet and 3% from structured open learning.

68.   The new ICT-equipped local learning centres, such as learndirect, register an encouraging 2% already, with 3% among 35-44s.

69.   In terms of widening participation, it is further education that currently reaches more people in the C2 (24%) and DE (31%) classes. They also provide for more rural dwellers (24%). The workplace plays a vital role in reaching skilled manual workers, 19% of whom are learning in the workplace. Twenty-two per cent of those giving work-related reasons for their study are learning in the workplace.

Length of study

70.   Fifty-eight per cent of those surveyed have been studying their main subject for more than a year, 4% for less than one week and 10% for less than a month. Nearly one third of learners are studying for three hours or less with 10% more women than men doing so. At the other end, more men than women are spending longer per week on their studies. Nearly 20% appear effectively to be studying full-time.

The role of qualifications

71. Two thirds of current/recent learners are aiming for a qualification, an increase of 2 per cent since 1999.

72.   Over 90% of 17-24-year-olds are aiming for a qualification. The proportion drops to 75% among 25-34-year-olds and then continues to decline steadily, though as many as 40% of 55-64-year-olds and 33% of 65-74-year-olds are still interested in a qualification.

73.   Two thirds of both men and women are aiming for a qualification (66%), although more men than women report studying for a degree (14% compared with 10%) and for level 4/5 qualifications more generally (30% compared with 28%).

74.   Seventeen to twenty-four-year-olds are mainly aiming for A-levels, NVQs or a first degree. Older adults of working age are mainly aiming for NVQs, professional and other qualifications, while some also continuing to aim towards more traditional qualifications such as City and Guilds. Unemployed adults are mainly aiming for NVQ/SVQs (23%).

Qualifications and the national learning targets

75.   Twenty-eight per cent of respondents do not have any qualifications at all, roughly the same proportion as in 1996 and 1999. *a national failure!*

76.   Sixty-one per cent of respondents hold qualifications up to level 2, 37% up to level 3 and 24% up to levels 4 and 5.

77.   If 17-19-year-olds, many of whom are full-time students, and those beyond working age are both excluded from the survey totals, 69% of respondents hold qualifications up to level 2, 42% up to level 3 and 28% up to level 4.

78.   Although not an official measure of these targets, the results offer an indication of progress towards current government targets and enable an assessment of their impact upon different groups of adults. The results indicate that the current level 4 target is likely to have been achieved, but that the government is still short of its level 3 target.

79.   The new targets recently published for 2004 charge the Learning and Skills Councils with raising the proportion of adults, between the ages of 18 and 59/64 who are in employment or actively seeking it, with a level 3 qualifications to 52%. The LSC has also been charged with raising the achievement of the entire adult population, measured by the proportion attaining a level 3 qualification, and the proportion lacking the basic skills of literacy and numeracy, as well as with raising adult participation in learning. Details of the new targets are to be published shortly.

Motivations for learning

80.   When questioned on why they were learning their chosen subject, 62% of respondents cited personal development reasons, 53% work-related reasons, and 27% cited education/progression reasons. Six per cent said that participation in their main learning activity was not really their choice.

81.   The most frequently cited individual reasons for learning their main subject were: 'I am interested in the subject/personal interest' (34%), and 'I enjoy learning/it gives me pleasure' (31%). Around a quarter of respondents mentioned 'to help in my current job' (26%), 'to develop myself as a person' (25%), and 'to get a recognised qualification' (24%).

82.   Adults are rarely motivated to learn by just a single factor, but will often only begin learning when a range of factors come together. For example, two thirds of those who identified education/progression reasons for starting learning also cited personal development and work-related reasons.

Attitudes to learning

83.   Eighty-one per cent of adults believe that aside from the instrumental benefits that it can bring, 'learning is enjoyable for its own sake'.

84.   Nearly three quarters of respondents (74%) say that they are 'confident about learning new skills'. This rises to 92% of current learners but is down to 55% among those who have not engaged in any learning since leaving full-time education.

85.   Seventy-four per cent agree that 'people who get training find their jobs are more interesting', while two thirds (66%) agree that 'people who get trained at work end up with better promotion or pay'.

86.   The continuing decline in the proportion of adults 'agreeing that there is not enough help and advice available about the different sorts of learning people can do' is encouraging. This figure fell from 47% in 1996, to 40% in 1999 and is now down to 37% in 2002.

87.   On the negative side, forty-seven per cent of respondents 'don't see why they should pay for learning that is to do with their job or career' while 32% believe that they 'should not be expected to learn new skills for their careers in their own time'. Adults who have not participated in any learning since leaving full-time education are most likely to hold these views.

Life circumstances

88.   Participation in adult learning can be related to major life changes and events. Wanting promotion at work (67%), starting a new job/being promoted (66%), moving home (60%) and a broken marriage/breaking up with a partner (54%) all relate to groups with higher proportions of current/recent learners than in the population as a whole.

89.   Over half (53%) of those who 'want to help their children learn' are themselves adult learners, compared to 42% overall. This represents a 5% increase since 1999.

Benefits of learning

90.   Adult learners experience a complex variety of benefits from their learning, some of which are connected to their original motivations for learning. Many learners are still in the course of their studies and may have experienced the short-term benefits, but not the long-term instrumental ones, such as job change.

91.   The most frequently cited benefits occurring or expected as a result of learning are improvements in self-confidence (29%), personal development (29%), meeting new people and making new friends (26%), and gaining a qualification (21%).

92.   Between 5-15% of respondents refer to experiencing or expecting a range of work-related benefits, from finding work more satisfying (15%) and being helped in their current job (14%), to getting a job with a different employer (5%).

93.   One in every six respondents (16%) reports not having experienced, or not expecting to experience, any benefit from their learning.

Barriers to learning

94.   Lack of intrinsic motivation continues to be a major barrier. A quarter of those who are not very likely to learn in the future say this is because they are not interested. This rises to 38% among those with few or no qualifications; to 37% among those who have not done any learning since leaving full-time education; to 35% of retired adults and those aged 55 and over; and 31% of those who left school at the earliest opportunity.

95.   Those adults who have not participated in any learning since leaving full-time education include 37% who are not interested/don't want to; 17% who feel too old; 15% who are prevented by work or other time pressures; and 11% who feel no need to learn any more.

96.   Four-fifths of current/recent learners (79%) say that they find it easy to get to where their learning takes place. A further 13% say that because their learning takes place at home or at work, they don't have to travel. Only 7% of current/recent learners say that it is difficult to get to where their learning takes place.

Funding of learning

97.   The proportion of learners who do not have to pay any fees has risen slightly from 26% in 1999 to 28% in 2002. A third of learners pay their own fees, with an additional 6% being helped by family members, twice the figure from 1999.

98.   Of those with fees to pay, more women (36%) than men (30%) pay their own fees, while more men (25%) than women (18%) have fees paid by their employer.

99.   Employer support for outside fees is stronger for full-time workers (24%) than for part-time workers (13%), although the gap has been reduced by 5% since 1999.

100. Three times as many full-time (12%) as part-time (4%) workers benefit from employer funded provision of learning.

101. The proportion of full-time students paying their own fees has virtually doubled over the past three years from 11% to 20%, while the proportion receiving local authority grants has fallen considerably from 42% to 13%.

102. Adults at either end of the age spectrum are least likely to have to pay fees, either because at the younger end they still remain within initial education for which no fees apply, or because of fee remission at the older end.

103. One half of all learners, both men and women, say that their learning has not resulted in any additional costs. This figure represents an increase of seven points since 1999.

104. The two most significant additional costs are travel costs (31%) and costs of equipment (28%).

The information divide: an update

105. Forty-one per cent of respondents report regular access to the internet. This is a three-fold increase since the 1999 survey. However, the demographic differences between regions, age and socio-economic classes continue to be dramatic. Three quarters (76%) of the upper classes (AB) have regular access to a computer but only 51% of the skilled working class (C2s) and less than one third (28%) of the unskilled working class and those on benefit.

106. Computers and phone lines still act as the most important gateway to the internet since all but 2% continue to access the internet through a computer. Five per cent say they have access to a broadband connection.

107. More men than women continue to have access to a computer/pc, (by 7%) and to the internet, (by 9%). Socio-economic class still shows a major divide, with two thirds (67%) of ABs having regular access to the internet; 55% of C1s; 36% of C2s; and 17% of DEs.

108. The proportion of respondents who have regular access to the internet reaches 50% or over for all the age-groups up to 45, but then drops to 48% for 45-54s; 32% for 55-64s; 14% for 65-74s; and 4% for 75+.

109. While there is no difference between rural and urban areas (both 41%) the differences between nations range from 41% in England to 36% in Wales, and between the regions of England, from 48% in the North-East and South-East to 37 % in the West Midlands and 34% in the North-West.

110. The best-connected group to the internet are parents of children aged 5-15 (56%).

111. The internet is still mostly used for e-mail (37%) and general browsing/surfing (21%). Six per cent mostly use it for finding information for their own learning, and this rises to 12% among current learners. A further 2% use it mostly for learning on/off line and 3% for finding information for their children's schoolwork.

112. While these signs of educational use are encouraging, access barriers are still great as is the continuing risk of increasing the information divide, particularly between the young and the old as well as between the upper and lower classes.

CHAPTER ONE

Trends in leisure and lifestyle

In this sequence of studies of adult learning, which now covers 20 years, we have continued to focus on 'leisure', since this is the time in which the vast majority of adults choose to undertake much of their active learning. The Oxford English Dictionary's definition of leisure is helpful: 'Freedom or opportunity to do something specific or implied', and in the narrower sense, 'opportunity afforded by freedom from occupation'. Participation in learning is, for adults, a matter of choice, and has to be fitted in with work, family and other interests and obligations. Increasingly, many people are also learning in the workplace, whether to help with their work or for personal reasons. For some people the boundaries between leisure and learning are virtually invisible. Frequently, leisure activities provide a bridge into active learning.

A further proposition is that leisure activities can often involve informal learning, which may or may not be recognised as such by the learner. Tough's classic work *The adult's learning projects* (1971) suggests that almost everyone undertakes one or two major learning efforts a year, and some individuals undertake as many as 15 or 20; and that about 70% of all learning projects are planned by learners themselves. His work, though much quoted, has sadly not been replicated in this country and his style of questioning cannot easily be incorporated into a regular pattern of large-scale social surveys such as these. However, changing leisure patterns and lifestyle habits offer some indications of changes in behaviour.

The use of leisure is affected by opportunity, and social changes are combining with technological changes to expand some opportunities while others are being contracted or even closed down. This chapter focuses on trends in leisure interests and use of social, cultural and community resources, drawing on national studies in 1980, 1990 and 2002. A parallel study *Learning for a purpose* (1993) using similar questions was carried out among the main ethnic groups resident in Great Britain in 1992.

Viewing and listening of television and radio has not been included in this sequence of studies since it is documented by the industry in great detail. People spend over three-and-a-half-hours a day watching television on average. It is important to remember that people still spend more time on viewing television than they do on any other activity except sleeping and working (if they are in work). Men have more leisure-time than women and this gap is widening as many more women have now entered the labour-market and still have to cope with the double agenda of work and family.

The proportions recording social activities as their main leisure activity have remained stable across the 20 years, at between 44% to 46%. Reading, which dominated the list both in 1980 (48%) and 1990 (51%) has dropped to 41% but is still the most important activity among women (51%) in 2002. Sports and physical activities now have equal ranking with reading at 41%, though men engage in sports more frequently than women (49% compared with 35%). Sports and physical activities showed a big increase between 1980 and 1990, from 34% to 40% and are now stable. In 1980 and 1990, DIY, handicrafts, cookery, needlework and all the domestic arts and skills were grouped together. These have now been separated in 2002, showing the gender differences more clearly and recording an overall drop of 5% in such activities. At the same time, the proportion naming gardening has also dropped by 6%. Perhaps the success of popularised gardening programmes has turned more people into armchair gardeners and stopped them doing the real thing! (Table 1.1)

There also appears to be an unwelcome drop of 10% in the proportions mentioning voluntary/committee work. Most other activities have remained stable. In 1990 it was suggested that '...associated changes in subjects of learning indicated that these changes were more to do with a redefinition of sport as leisure rather than learning, and a redefinition of handicrafts/DIY as a domestic duty rather than as a leisure activity.'

An interim study in 1996 (*The Learning Divide*, 1996) asked a smaller group of people more detailed questions in relation to arts and crafts and separated the predominately male activities of handicrafts/DIY from the predominately female activities of sewing, knitting etc. The joint group recorded 34% in 1990, a drop of 6% from 1980. The two groups together in 2002 show a similar drop of 5% from 1990. Sewing/knitting etc is very gender-specific with 1% only of men recording it as a main interest and among women the proportions increase with age. Handicrafts/DIY is less gender-specific with only 9% more men than women mentioning it. Four per cent of respondents in 2002 admit to having no main leisure interest, only 1% more than in 1990 and 1980.

Table 1.1: Main leisure activities and interests, 1980, 1990 and 2002 compared

	Total	1980 Men	Women	Total	1990 Men	Women	Total	2000 Men	Women
Base: all respondents = 100%	2448	1196	1252	4246	1956	2290	4896	2381	2515
Social activities	44	44	44	46	50	43	45	43	47
Sports/physical activities	34	44	25	40	49	32	41	49	35
Reading	48	41	55	51	40	61	41	32	51
Gardening	33	33	33	34	33	34	28	26	30
DIY/handicrafts#	40	28	51	34	24	43	18	23	14
Sewing/knitting etc.		NSR			NSR		11	1	21
Creative arts: painting, writing etc.		NA			NA		11	10	11
Going to church/mosque etc.		NA			NA		7	5	9
Indoor games: e.g. chess, bridge	11	14	10	11	14	9	7	9	6
Voluntary service/ committee work##	6	5	7	16	13	18	13	11	15
Collecting: e.g. stamps	4	5	4	5	7	3	NA	NA	NA
Performing music	6	7	5	5	6	3	5	7	4
Other interests		NSR		7	7	6	8	10	7
None	3	3	3	3	4	3	4	4	4

DIY/handicrafts were grouped together in 1990. In the 1996 Arts and Crafts Survey, sewing, knitting etc were recorded separately at 12% with DIY at 7%.
Voluntary service and committee work have been grouped together in 2002.
NA = not asked
NSR = not separately recorded

Some leisure activities and interests are related to age, family position and location. Table 1.2 shows main leisure activities and interests by age and demonstrates the age trends very strongly. Not surprisingly, social activities and sports figure more highly among the young, while gardening and sewing/knitting increase gradually with age. It is encouraging that reading still maintains a significant proportion across all age groups as does DIY/handicrafts among all but the upper and lower age-groups. Included for the first time as a main activity is the importance of places of worship, which also increases with age as does involvement in voluntary work. Also separated out for the first time, as leisure activities, are the creative arts, which rank at 10% or more across all the age-groups except those aged 75+.

Table 1.2: Main leisure activities and interests, apart from television and radio, by age

	Total	17-19	20-24	25-34	35-44	45-54	55-64	65-74	75+
Base: all respondents = 100%	4896	250	336	887	1002	757	705	583	375
Social activities	45	63	66	56	48	42	37	32	19
Sports/physical activities	41	50	54	52	46	40	38	28	18
Reading	41	28	39	41	37	41	46	47	50
Gardening	28	2	4	15	26	37	42	42	34
DIY/handicrafts#	18	6	10	18	24	25	21	14	9
Sewing/knitting etc.	11	3	3	6	9	14	15	17	18
Creative arts: painting, writing etc.*	11	14	11	10	10	13	11	12	7
Going to church/mosque etc.	7	2	4	4	5	8	11	11	15
Indoor games: e.g. chess, bridge	7	7	10	9	7	6	6	8	6
Voluntary service/committee work##	6	2	4	3	5	7	9	7	8
Performing music	5	12	10	6	4	5	4	4	1
Other interests	8	6	8	6	8	7	11	12	9
None mentioned	4	3	2	4	3	4	5	5	8

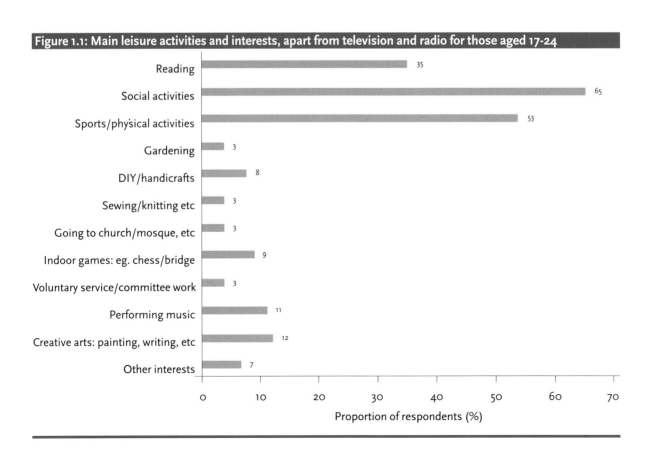

Figure 1.1: Main leisure activities and interests, apart from television and radio for those aged 17-24

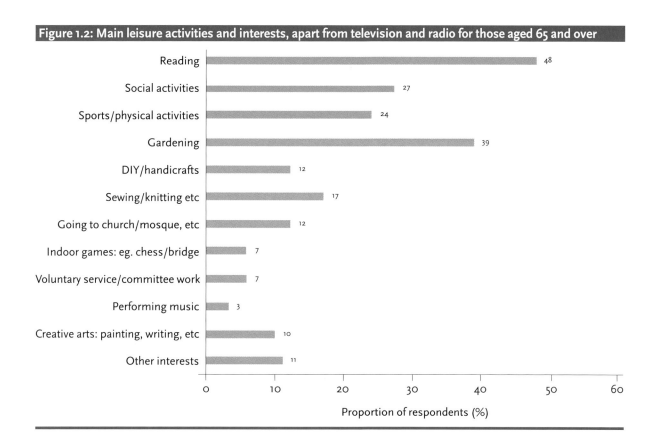

Figure 1.2: Main leisure activities and interests, apart from television and radio for those aged 65 and over

Table 1.3: Main leisure activities and interests, apart from television and radio, by socio-economic group and by type of area

	Total	Social Class				Type of area	
		AB	C1	C2	DE	Rural	Urban
Base: all respondents = 100%	4896	906	1398	1084	1509	895	4001
Social activities	45	50	51	47	35	37	47
Sports/physical activities	41	53	47	42	28	44	41
Reading	41	54	44	33	37	36	43
Gardening	28	34	29	27	24	31	27
DIY/handicrafts	18	23	20	20	13	18	18
Sewing/knitting etc.	11	11	10	10	12	12	11
Creative arts: painting, writing etc.	11	18	12	8	7	10	11
Going to church/mosque etc.	7	12	8	5	5	7	7
Indoor games: e.g. chess/ bridge	7	8	9	7	5	6	7
Voluntary service/ committee work	6	11	7	3	3	6	6
Performing music	5	8	7	4	3	5	5
Other interests	8	8	8	8	9	10	8
None mentioned	4	1	2	5	7	3	4

Figure 1.3: Main leisure activities, apart from television and radio, by type of area

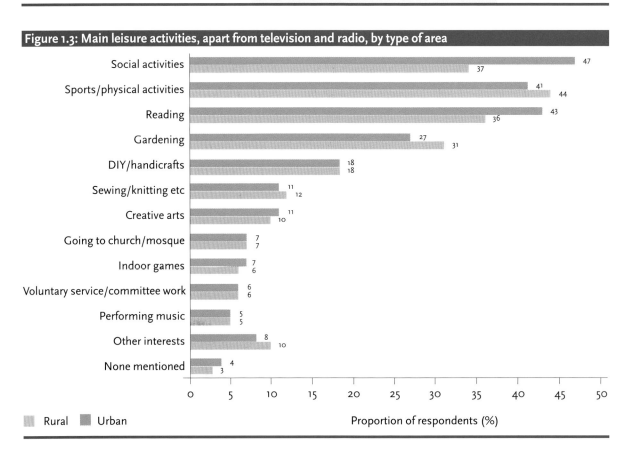

Rural Urban   Proportion of respondents (%)

Table 1.3 shows main leisure interests analysed by socio-economic class and by whether people live in urban or rural areas. Going down the classes from AB to DE, virtually every activity shows a drop in the proportion mentioning them. The only exceptions to this are reading and sewing/knitting *etc* which increase slightly among DEs. Of course the DE group contains a large number of pensioners, particularly women. However, it is counter-intuitive to find fewer C2s and even C1s engaging in social activities and in sport, for example. While some activities such as the arts and voluntary service are seen as more likely to be engaged in by upper- and middle-class people, the descending graph for church-going is less obvious. While finance may affect some activities, it is obviously not the only explanation.

Gardening is similarly a joker, as it also descends with social class, but then many people in urban areas do not have gardens of their own, and gardening ranks 4% higher among rural dwellers than it does among urban dwellers. Urban dwellers read more and engage more in social activities while rural dwellers engage more in gardening and physical activities. Apart from this there is no effective difference in leisure activities between the two groups.

Table 1.4: Main leisure activities and interests, apart from television and radio, by ethnicity

| | Total | Ethnicity | | | |
		Black	Asian	Other	White
Base: all respondents = 100%	4896	114	180	51	4544
Social activities	45	35	45	48	45
Sports/physical activities	41	47	32	36	42
Reading	41	41	42	41	41
Gardening	28	14	12	20	29
DIY/handicrafts	18	10	9	7	19
Sewing/knitting etc.	11	5	8	4	11
Creative arts: painting, writing etc.	11	10	10	13	11
Going to church/mosque etc.	7	5	9	7	7
Indoor games: e.g. chess/bridge	7	5	7	6	7
Voluntary service/committee work	6	5	3	2	6
Performing music	5	7	6	3	5
Other interests	8	6	7	9	8
None mentioned	4	7	8	7	4

Figure 1.4: Main leisure activities and interests, apart from television and radio, by ethnicity

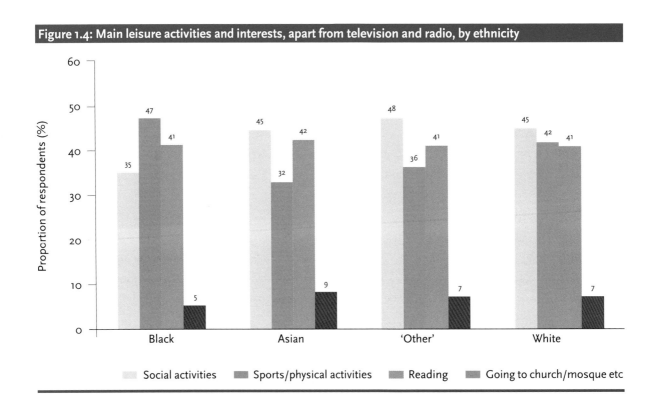

Table 1.5: Main leisure activities and interests, apart from television and radio, by learning status

	Total	Current	Learning Status Recent	In past	Never	Future Learning Likely	Not likely
Base: all respondents = 100%	4896	1130	943	1039	1747	1986	2777
Social activities	45	56	51	42	36	53	39
Sports/physical activities	41	55	47	39	31	50	35
Reading	41	47	43	45	35	44	40
Gardening	28	24	27	32	29	24	31
DIY/handicrafts	18	21	22	20	13	22	16
Sewing/knitting etc.	11	8	10	12	12	10	11
Creative arts: painting, writing etc.	11	19	13	10	5	15	8
Going to church/mosque etc.	7	11	6	8	5	7	7
Indoor games: e.g. chess/bridge	7	10	9	8	4	9	6
Voluntary service/committee work	6	10	7	7	2	7	5
Performing music	5	9	7	4	2	8	3
Other interests	8	8	8	9	8	9	8
None mentioned	4	1	2	3	7	2	5

While the size of individual ethnic groups appearing in the sample is small, they represent the national proportions and do justify separating into three groups: black, Asian and 'other'. (Table 1.4.) The black group ranks sports and physical activities highest, at 47%, followed by reading (41%) and social activities (35%). The Asian group, the largest, places social activities highest (45%), followed by reading (42%) and then sporting and physical activities (32%). The 'other' category places social activities highest (48%), followed by reading (41%) and sports (36%). The next highest activities for all three ethnic groups are gardening, DIY/handicrafts and creative arts. Of all the groups, the Asian group puts 'place of worship' the highest, at 9%.

Main leisure activity and interests related to learning

Completing this section, Table 1.5 analyses main leisure activities and interests against respondents' current study status, and their likelihood of learning in the next three years. It makes clear those activities which are strongly related to current learning status and the likelihood of future learning and those activities which appear not to be related. A higher proportion of current learners also engage in social activities (56%), in sports and physical activities (55%), in reading (47%) and in creative arts (19%). Many other activities reduce among less-active or non-learners. The activities which do not vary much according to learning status are reading,

Table 1.6: Frequency of use of cultural and community facilities: 1980, 1990 and 2002 compared

Base: all respondents = 100%	1980 Total	Men	Women	1990 Total	Men	Women	2002 Total	Men	Women
Public library visited									
At least once a week or more often	14	12	16	11	10	12	10	9	10
Less than once a week to once a month	24	22	27	23	20	26	24	12	26
Less often/never	61	66	57	67	71	64	65	69	61
Cinema visited									
At least once a week or more often	2	2	1	1	1	1	4	4	3
Less than once a week to once a month	12	13	10	14	16	12	29	30	28
Less often/never	87	85	89	85	83	87	67	66	69
Theatre visited									
At least once a week or more often	*	*	*	*	*	1	1	1	*
Less than one a week to once a month	6	6	6	6	5	7	9	8	10
Less often/never	94	94	94	93	95	92	90	91	89
Concert/opera/ballet attended									
At least once a week or more often	*	1	*	1	1	*	*	*	*
Less than once a week to once a month	7	7	7	6	8	5	9	9	8
Less often/never	93	93	93	93	92	94	91	91	91
Places of worship attended									
At least once a week or more often	13	10	16	13	10	16	14	12	17
Less than once a week to once a month	10	7	12	9	7	11	8	7	9
Less often/never	77	82	73	78	83	73	78	82	74

gardening and DIY/handicrafts, with sewing/knitting actually increasing marginally among non-learners. In general, activity seems to breed activity.

Cultural activities and the use of community facilities

The concept of social capital is now back on the political agenda, and Bourdieu's theories are back in fashion with sociologists. The inter-relationship of educational and social capital is of importance in the debate on social inclusion, and the survey also provides some markers over the two decades of cultural and community access. Table 1.6 compares visits made to public libraries, cinemas, theatres, concerts and places of worship in 1980, 1990 and 2002. The 1996

Table 1.7a: Proportion engaging in listed activities at least once a month									
	Total	17-19	20-24	25-34	35-44	45-54	55-64	65-74	75+
Base: all respondents = 100%	4896	250	336	887	1002	757	705	583	375
Visit public library	35	44	42	34	36	33	31	35	33
Go to cinema	32	72	72	53	37	23	14	7	4
Go to theatre	10	14	11	10	9	10	11	9	4
Go to concert/opera/ballet	9	15	15	10	7	9	8	7	6
Go to place of worship	22	20	18	16	19	21	28	27	35
Go to a museum	9	9	12	10	12	9	7	7	5
Go to an art gallery	6	9	10	7	6	7	5	7	3
Go to community centre/social club	23	23	28	21	18	23	24	25	26

Arts and Crafts survey also asked about museums, art galleries and community centres and these were also included in the 2002 survey (Table 1.7a).

Public libraries continue to play a significant role in offering gateways to learning through books and increasingly through other media. Their funding came under great pressure for a decade or more as local authority funding was being cut back and many areas closed libraries or reduced their hours and it was not surprising that the 1990 survey recorded a drop of 4% in their regular use. This downward trend appears to have stopped and is likely to reflect the increased funding and emphasis under the current libraries improvement programme and the People's Network. Many libraries have already been kitted up with ICT and have extended their role in relation to learning, for example offering access to learndirect. This offers encouragement for their future particularly in relation to learning and ICT support.

Most encouraging is the level of use of libraries among young people, with 44% of 17-19-year-olds and 42% of 20-24-year-olds using them at least once a month. Also encouraging is that 22% of black and 21% of Asian people visit public libraries at least once a week, twice the percentage of the general population. Libraries are, however, more used by the upper- (41%) and middle-classes (39%) and their use drops to 30% among C2s and DEs (Table 1.7b).

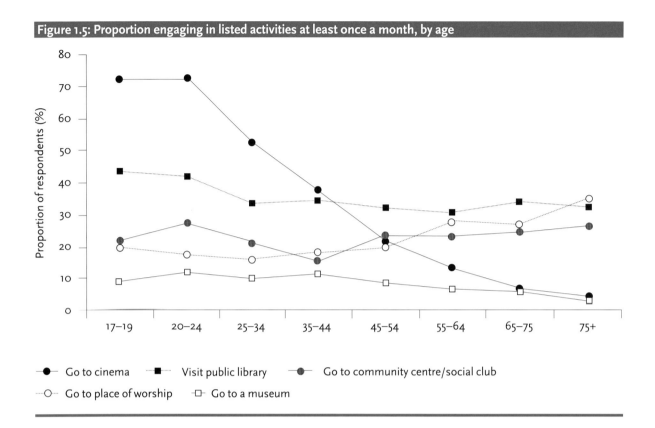

Figure 1.5: Proportion engaging in listed activities at least once a month, by age

Table 1.7b: Proportion engaging in listed activities at least once a month, by socio-economic group

	Total	AB	C1	C2	DE
Base: all respondents = 100%	4896	906	1398	1084	1509
Visit public library	35	41	39	29	32
Go to cinema	32	38	40	32	22
Go to theatre	10	16	14	7	4
Go to concert/opera/ballet	9	16	11	7	4
Go to place of worship	22	31	24	17	19
Go to a museum	9	15	11	7	5
Go to an art gallery	9	11	7	4	4
Go to community centre/ social club	23	22	22	22	24

The inter-relationship with educational level is illustrated clearly, for example, with the highest level of those using public libraries at least once a month, being individuals whose education continued until the age of 21 or over (Table 1.7c).

Table 1.7c: Proportion engaging in listed activities at least once a month, by terminal age of education					
	Total	Up to 16	17-18	19-20	21 and over
Base: all respondents = 100%	4896	2899	766	207	798
Visit public library	35	29	38	32	46
Go to cinema	32	23	41	42	44
Go to theatre	10	6	11	14	18
Go to concert/opera/ballet	9	5	11	10	18
Go to place of worship	22	18	25	29	31
Go to a museum	9	6	10	9	18
Go to an art gallery	6	3	6	9	15
Go to community centre/ social club	23	24	22	19	20

Cinemas are enjoying a major resurgence of interest with one third of all respondents visiting them at least once a month. There is a small increase in those going at least once a week from 1% to 4%, and twice the number of people increasing their visits from once a week to once a month. Cinema-going is predominantly an activity of the young with 72% of the youngest age-groups going at least once a month, then the proportions drop dramatically with increasing age. Sixteen per cent of 17-19-year-olds and 14% of 20-24-year-olds go to the cinema each week. C1s are the socio-economic class that goes to the cinema most (40%) but even one in five (22%) of the unskilled working class go at least once a month (22%).

Figure 1.6: Proportion engaging in listed activities at least once a month, by socio-economic group

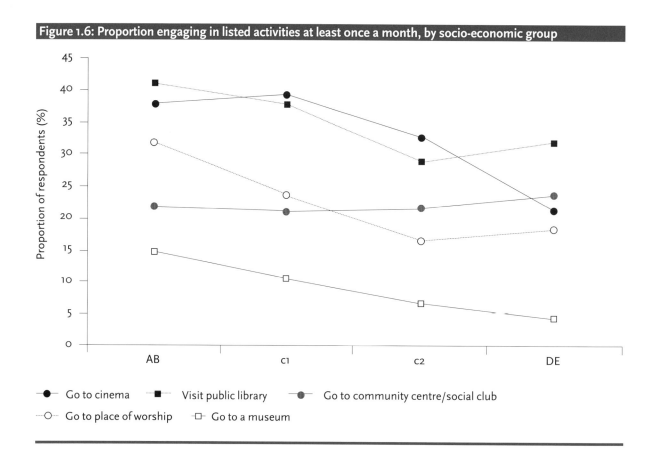

It is encouraging that theatre-going has also increased since 1990, from 6% of respondents going at least once a month in 1990, increasing to 10%, with a small number (2%) of women going more often than men. The theatre, unlike the cinema, follows the expected pattern of the upper and middle classes going more often than the lower socio-economic classes, with the same inter-related dominance of the better-educated. The people who go to operas/concerts/ballet tend to be younger, tend to be more upper class and better educated.

Table 1.8: Frequency of use of cultural and community facilities: 1996 and 2002 compared					
		1996			2002	
	Total	Men	Women	Total	Men	Women
Base: all respondents = 100%	2022	983	1039	4896	2381	2515
Attended social club/community centre						
At least once a week or more often	13	15	11	13	14	12
Less than once a week to once a month	12	12	11	10	11	9
Less often/never	75	73	78	77	75	79
Attended museum						
At least once a week or more often	1	1	*	1	1	*
Less than once a week to once a month	8	8	8	8	9	8
Less often/never	92	92	91	91	90	92
Attended art gallery						
At least once a week or more often	1	1	*	*	1	*
Less than once a week to once a month	7	6	7	6	6	6
Less often/never	93	93	93	94	93	94

Visits to a concert or opera were grouped in both 1980 and 1990, and the 2002 survey also added ballet into this group. These more specialist activities together attract 9% of respondents to them at least once a month, with 1% of these going at least once a week. Two other cultural activities were added in 1996 through the Arts and Crafts survey, 'attending museums' and 'art galleries'. Despite the extra attention and resources provided to museums, this had not yet resulted in an increase in attendance and the proportions in 2002 are virtually the same as in 1996. The recent introduction of free admission to museums is likely to have a positive impact on this.

Also added in 1996 as an indicator of diversity, was attendance at a social club or community centre. Nearly one-quarter of respondents say they attend such a venue at least once a month, and the proportion has stayed about the same as in 1996.

Table 1.9a: Proportion engaging in listed activities at least once a month, by learning status

Base: all respondents = 100%	Total	Current learners	Recent learners	Past learners	Never
Visit public library	35	51	36	33	25
Go to cinema	32	51	40	27	20
Go to community centre/ social club	23	26	23	20	22
Go to place of worship	22	28	20	24	18

Table 1.9b: Proportion engaging in listed activities at least once a month, by learning status

Base: all respondents = 100%	Total	Current learners	Recent learners	Past learners	Never
Go to theatre	10	15	13	8	6
Go to concert/opera/ballet	9	16	11	7	4
Go to a museum	9	16	9	7	5
Go to an art gallery	6	13	6	6	3

Finally in this section Tables 1.9a and 1.9b analyse regular participation in these activities by current learning status. In the previous section, the link between initial length of education and use of community and cultural resources was made clear, as was its inter-relationship with socio-economic class. Tables 1.9a and 1.9b add the link with current learning activity. Perhaps surprisingly, current learners engage in every single activity, whether specifically cultural or not, at higher rates than recent, past or non-learners. One half (51%) of current learners also visit public libraries once a month, and go to the cinema at least once a month. Twenty-eight per cent of current learners go to a place of worship and 26% to a community centre/social club at least once a month. Recent, past and non-learners engage in all these activities at declining rates. The table has been reordered in two parts, with the four more common activities in Table 1.9a and the specialist arts activities in Table 1.9b. Either way, the links between cultural capital and educational capital are clear.

CHAPTER TWO

Current and recent participation in adult learning

Measuring participation

For over a decade, NIACE has undertaken a series of surveys to measure adult participation in learning.[1] These surveys have not only provided information on the proportion of adults participating in learning and a detailed breakdown of who participates and who does not, but the comparison of results within the series, enables the examination of how patterns of participation change over time.

Previous surveys were carried out in 1990, 1996 and 1999 and the same introductory question has been used since 1996. This question has been drafted as broadly as possible to include all types of learning and in any mode. It is a question asked of individuals themselves, not in terms of levels or providers, and it asks the respondents to answer the question "which of the following statements most applies to you?". This question was originally developed by SCPR for the Employment Department in 1993 as offering a broader view of learning than earlier surveys, and NIACE agreed to adopt it in 1996 in order to improve comparability and establish trend data. For those unfamiliar with the question, it is repeated here.

> "I would now like to talk about the sort of learning that people do. Learning can mean practising, studying or reading about something. It can also mean being taught, instructed or coached. This is so you can develop skills, knowledge, abilities or understanding of something. Learning can also be called education or training. You can do it regularly (each day or month) or you can do it for a short period of time. It can be full-time or part-time, done at home, at work, or in another place like a college. Learning does not have to lead to a qualification. We are interested in any learning you have done, whether or not it was finished."

---

[1] This series builds upon an initial survey undertaken by ACACE in 1980, *Adults: their educational experience and needs.*

Which of the following statements most applies to you?

01: I am currently doing some learning activity

02: I have done some learning activity in the last three years

03: I have studied or learned but it was over three years ago

04: I have not studied or learned since I left full-time education

05: Don't know

This chapter seeks to illustrate how patterns of participation in learning have changed over the last decade or so, using the results of the 1990, 1996, 1999 and 2002 surveys.

Trends in participation in learning in relation to gender

The 2002 survey shows that nearly one in four adults (23%) are currently learning, with 42% of adults having participated in some learning activity during the last three years. This represents a steady increase of two per cent since the 1996 and 1999 surveys, when 40% of adults said that they were current or recent learners.

Other NIACE-commissioned surveys, undertaken in 2000 and 2001 reported current/recent participation figures of 41% and 46% respectively. The results of these two surveys are not included in the tables within this report, although they are referred to in the text where relevant. The reason for this is that in both 2000 and 2001 only two questions from the major surveys were asked – one on participation in learning and the other on future intentions to learn – thus data on the full range of questions covered in this report are not available for these years. The findings from the 2000 and 2001 surveys are included in the report *Two steps forward, one step back* (Aldridge and Tuckett, NIACE, 2002) which outlines the headline findings of the 2002 survey, as well as comparing patterns of participation from all the surveys conducted since 1996.

Table 2.1: Current/recent learning by gender, 1990, 1996, 1999 and 2002 compared				
	1990	1996	1999	2002
	Proportion studying now/ recently and/or learning informally	Proportion who are current/recent learners		
Total sample	39	40	40	42
Men	42	43	41	43
Women	36	38	40	42

NB Percentages are horizontal

The NIACE series of participation surveys has always shown that men are more likely to participate in learning than women, however the proportion of women learners has increased over time such that, for the first time in 2002, men and women are currently participating in equal numbers, although more women (39%) than men (34%) say that they have not done any learning since leaving full-time education. This may be influenced in part by the higher proportion of older women in the adult population, many of whom will have had limited opportunities for learning in their youth, as well as by the increasing presence of women in the workforce, and the steady decline in the proportion of men at work – since work remains a major location of learning.

Table 2.2: Participation in learning, men and women compared

	Total	Men	Women
Base: all respondents = 100%	4896	2381	2515
Current learning	23	23	23
Recent learning (in the last 3 years)	19	19	19
All current/recent learning	42	43	42
Past learning (more than 3 years ago)	21	23	19
None since leaving full-time education/don't know	36	34	39

Trends in participation in learning in relation to socio-economic class

Socio-economic class remains a key determinant of adult participation in learning. The six categories that are commonly used are described briefly below, with a fuller description provided in Appendix 2. Grade A includes the upper and upper-middle classes and is generally grouped with Grade B the middle classes. Grade C1 includes the lower-middle class, often called white-collar workers. Grade C2 mainly consists of skilled manual workers. Grade D comprises the semi-skilled and unskilled working class, and is usually linked with Grade E, those on the lowest levels of subsistence such as old-age pensioners and those dependent upon welfare benefits.

The 2002 survey shows that a substantial divide remains between participation among the upper and middle classes, with three fifths of ABs and just over a half of C1s participating, compared with two fifths of C2s (skilled manual workers) and only a quarter of unskilled workers and people on limited incomes (DE). As a result, adults in socio-economic groups AB are more than twice as likely to be current or recent learners as those in groups DE. Furthermore, 58% of DEs have not participated in any learning since leaving school compared with just 17% of ABs (Table 2.3).

Table 2.3: Participation in learning, by socio-economic class

	Total	AB	C1	C2	DE
Base: all respondents = 100%	4896	906	1398	1084	1509
Current learning	23	35	32	17	12
Recent learning (in last 3 years)	19	25	22	19	13
All current/recent learning	42	60	54	37	25
Past learning (more than 3 years ago)	21	23	22	25	17
None since full-time education/don't know	36	17	24	39	58

The picture over time is no more encouraging (Table 2.4). Although since 1999, participation in learning has increased across all socio-economic groups, in just over a decade participation among the upper and middle classes has increased (from 54% to 60% of ABs; from 50% to 54% of C1s), while it has decreased slightly (from 38% to 37%) among skilled workers (C2) and remained constant at 25% among the least skilled (DE). In addition, when considering only those adults who are currently learning, the 2002 survey shows that participation levels, compared with the 1996 and 1999 surveys, remain unchanged for all groups except ABs, which show small increases in participation with each successive survey (Table 2.5).

Table 2.4: Current/recent learning by socio-economic class, 1990, 1996, 1999 and 2002 compared

	1990	1996	1999	2002
	Proportion studying now/ recently and/or learning informally	Proportion who are current/recent learners		
Total sample	39	40	40	42
A/B	54	53	58	60
C1	50	52	51	54
C2	38	33	36	37
DE	25	26	24	25

NB Percentages are horizontal

Table 2.5: Current learning by socio-economic class: 1990, 1996, 1999 and 2002 compared				
	1990	1996	1999	2002
	Proportion studying and/ or learning informally now	Proportion who are current learners		
Total sample	23	23	22	23
A/B	32	32	33	35
C1	31	32	32	32
C2	21	17	17	17
DE	15	12	12	12

NB Percentages are horizontal

Trends in participation in learning in relation to employment status

The workplace is not only a major location for learning, but also provides adults with information about learning opportunities, as well as the finance and motivation to take them up. Just over half of both full-time (52%) and part-time workers (51%) are current or recent learners, compared with 46% of the unemployed, 31% of those who are not working and just 19% of retired adults (Table 2.6). Around one half of those who are retired or who are not working say that they have not been involved in any learning since leaving full-time education.

Table 2.6: Participation in learning, by employment status						
	Total	Full-time	Part-time	Unemployed	Not working	Retired
Base: all respondents = 100%	4896	2008	566	187	739	1188
Current learning	23	25	28	17	13	11
Recent learning	19	26	23	29	17	8
All current/recent learning	42	52	51	46	31	19
Past learning	21	21	19	18	23	25
None since full-time education/don't know	36	27	30	35	47	56

Since the last major survey in 1999, the largest increase in learning has been among the unemployed, from 41% to 46%. This year's results also show that the substantial increases in participation achieved between the 1996 and 1999 surveys, among part-time workers and those who are not employed have also been further built upon and maintained respectively (Table 2.7). Since the 1990 survey was conducted, participation in learning has increased for all groups except the retired, where it has fallen slightly from 20% to 19%.

The high proportion of both full-time and part-time workers, and the increasing proportion of those who are classified as being unemployed and therefore seeking work, who are current/recent learners is perhaps not surprising given the national policy focus on learning as a means of improving the nation's economic competitiveness.

Table 2.7: Current/recent learning by employment status: 1990, 1996, 1999 and 2002 compared				
	1990	1996	1999	2002
	All current/recent and/ or informal learners	Proportion which are current/recent learners		
Total sample	39	40	40	42
Full-time	50	49	51	52
Part-time	42	42	50	51
Unemployed	39	40	41	46
Not working	24	23	31	31
Retired	20	20	16	19

NB Percentages are horizontal

Trends in participation in learning in relation to age and terminal age of education

The older people are, the less likely they are to participate in learning (Figure 2.1). Over 70% of those aged 17-24 are current or recent learners, compared with around half of those aged 25-54. The decline in participation becomes particularly steep for those aged 55 and over such that only 20% of adults aged 65-74 and 10% of those aged 75 and over regard themselves as learners.

Older people's participation in learning presents a significant challenge. The changing demography of the workforce and the increased longevity among retired groups both point to the need to foster participation in learning in later life, for work as well as to support a fulfilled and active life. Evidence from the Wider Benefits of Learning Research Centre, sponsored by the Department for Education and Skills points to a wide range of benefits from continuing in learning including benefits to health, to the family and for active citizenship (Schuller *et al* 2002). However, the continuing dominance of labour market concerns in education and skills policy seems unlikely to lead to concerted policy action to make a real difference to older people's learning opportunities – at least in the immediate future.

Figure 2.1: Current/recent participation in learning, by age

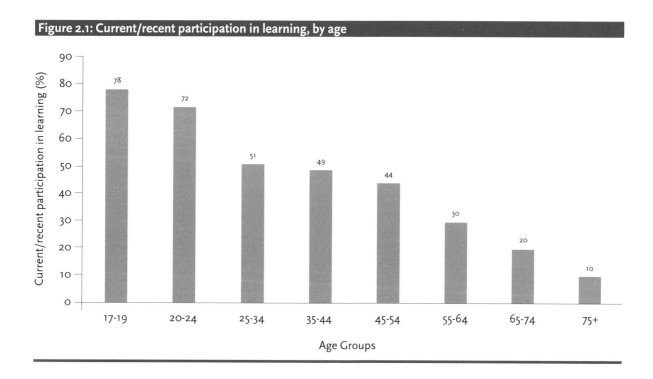

Table 2.8 compares the proportion of current/recent learners in each age group as found in the 1990, 1996, 1999 and 2002 surveys. The 1996 survey indicated that a reduction in labour market opportunities may have resulted in a significant rise in participation among 17-19-year-olds. In 1999, participation among this age group was shown to have fallen back. This fall continues into 2002, perhaps explained by the growth in numbers of young people at work. For most other age groups, levels of participation have been maintained or increased over the same period. Participation among those aged 75 and over has fallen.

Table 2.8 also shows in brackets the proportion of each age group who are in full-time education. A clear divide is evident between those under 25 where substantial numbers are studying full-time, and those aged 25 and over where only 2% or less of all other age groups are full-time students. This indicates a weakness in the debate over grants and fee policies for mature students which often fails to distinguish between full-time and part-time learners.

In 2002 the proportion of 17-19-year-olds in full-time education continued to fall, while an encouraging increase in the proportion of full-time learners aged 20-24 has resulted in the proportion of adults under 25 in full-time education remaining relatively stable. There has been no effective increase in the proportion of full-time students aged 25 and over in the last decade, and while the government target for 50% of young people to progress to higher education by the age of 30 by 2010 (DfES, 2001) is likely to lead to an increase in participation for younger adults, the price of this may well be even smaller proportions of older adults being able to benefit from such opportunities.

Table 2.8: Current/recent learning by age: 1990, 1996, 1999 and 2002 compared				
	1990	1996	1999	2002
	All current/recent and/ or informal learners	Proportion which are current/recent learners		
Total sample	39 (3)	40 (5)	40 (4)	42 (4)
17-19	63 (11)	86 (42)	81 (37)	78 (34)
20-24	66 (12)	65 (15)	70 (25)	72 (27)
25-34	46 (1)	48 (2)	50 (2)	51 (2)
35-44	43 (1)	43 (1)	47 (1)	49 (2)
45-54	35 (−)	36 (1)	41 (*)	44 (1)
55-64	23 (*)	25 (*)	30 (−)	30 (−)
65-74	15 (*)	19 (2)	16 (−)	20 (−)
75+		15 (−)	9 (−)	10 (−)

NB the proportion of full-time students in each group is shown in brackets. Percentages are horizontal

In previous surveys, terminal age of education has been a key predictor of participation in learning as an adult. This year's figures again confirm the key divide between those who leave school at the earliest opportunity and those who stay on even for a short while (Table 2.9). Only 30% of those who left school as early as possible are current/recent learners, compared with at least 45% of all other groups. However, Table 2.9 also shows that those who left full-time education aged 19-20 (45%) are less likely to be current/recent learners than both those who left aged 17-18 (52%) and those who left aged 21 and over (65%). The reason for this pattern, which has not been evident in previous surveys, is unclear.

Table 2.9: Participation in learning, by terminal age of education					
	Total	Up to 16	17-18	19-20	21+
Base: all respondents	4896	2899	766	207	798
Current learning	23	13	26	25	37
Recent learning	19	16	26	21	29
All current/recent learning	42	30	52	45	65
Past learning	21	21	25	31	22
None since full-time education/don't know	36	50	24	23	13

Trends in participation in learning in relation to nations and regions of the UK

Participation across the nations and regions of the UK continue to display considerable differences that cannot be easily explained. Devolution, which has taken place since the last major survey in 1999, has resulted in a shift of decision-making powers out to the Welsh and Scottish Assemblies and the adoption of different policies concerning lifelong learning. Chapters in *Adult Learning and Social Division: A Persistent Pattern Volume 2* by Stephen Gorard, Maria Slowey and John Field take a more detailed look at what the survey findings say about participation in Wales, Scotland and Northern Ireland respectively.

In April 2001 the national Learning and Skills Council, with its 47 local arms, was given responsibility for the funding and planning of all post-16 education and training in England, except for higher education, replacing both the Training and Enterprise Councils (TECs) and the Further Education Funding Council (FEFC). The wide remit of the LSC is intended in part to enable effective co-ordination and strategic planning at a national level in order to reduce uneven levels and quality of provision across England. This is balanced however, against the responsibility of local LSCs to ensure that the needs of local communities are reflected and met through LSC-funded provision. Other factors such as the demographic and social-class profile of different areas and differences in the availability and nature of educational and employment opportunities also have an impact upon national and regional participation rates.

Table 2.10: Participation in learning, by nation of the UK and type of area							
	Total	England	Wales	Scotland	Northern Ireland	Rural	Urban
Base: all respondents = 100%	4896	4036	241	475	144	895	4001
Current learning	23	23	19	25	20	21	24
Recent learning	19	19	20	19	20	20	19
All current/recent learning	42	42	39	44	40	41	43
Past learning	21	22	22	21	14	24	21
None since full-time education/don't know	36	36	39	35	47	35	37

In 2002, the highest proportion of current/recent learners is to be found in Scotland (44%), where participation has increased by 11% since 1999, and the lowest proportion in Wales, where it has fallen by 4%. While participation in Northern Ireland has risen by 8% to 40% this year, nearly a half of all adults in Northern Ireland report not having done any learning since leaving full-time education (Tables 2.10 and 2.11). It is necessary to remember the smaller sample sizes involved when examining data concerning Scotland and Northern Ireland, which should be interpreted with care. The sample for Wales was boosted to 995 for the 2002 survey, although it has been re-weighted for this report.

Despite an assumption that learners face greater barriers to learning in rural areas, Table 2.10 shows that participation in urban areas (43%) is only slightly higher than in rural ones (41%), confirming the pattern found in 1999.

Table 2.11: Current/recent learning by UK nation: 1996, 1999 and 2002 compared

	1996	1999	2002
Total sample	40	40	42
England	42	41	42
Wales	37	43	39
Scotland	38	33	44
Northern Ireland	28	32	40

NB Percentages are horizontal

Previous surveys have used standard regions for their analysis. Since the last major survey in 1999, the Government has established a new regional structure of nine Government Office regions. The majority of the regional boundaries have remained the same, but four have changed. The main differences are that Cumbria is now included within the North West region, with the Northern region being renamed the North East; while Essex, Hertfordshire and Bedfordshire are no longer included as part of the South East, but have been combined with counties in East Anglia to form a new Eastern region.

Table 2.12 shows participation in each of the English Government Office regions. Highest participation levels are reported in the South East (48%) and North East (46%). The North West (39%) and the Eastern region (36%) report the lowest levels of participation.

Table 2.12: Participation in learning, by Government Office region

	Total	North East	North West	Yorks & Humber	East Mids	West Mids	Eastern	London	South East	South West
Base: all respondents =100%	4896	276	639	518	431	471	401	498	477	326
Current learning	23	30	21	24	22	21	16	25	27	27
Recent learning	19	16	19	18	21	18	20	20	20	18
All current/ recent learning	42	46	39	41	44	40	36	45	48	45
Past learning	21	22	24	21	25	19	22	14	25	22
None since full-time education/don't know	36	33	36	37	32	41	42	42	27	33

Table 2.13 shows the same data for standard regions, as used in previous surveys, and indicates that since 1990 there have been considerable regional swings in participation, although with the exception of the West Midlands and East Anglia, participation levels have risen overall. Since 1999, the greatest regional increases in participation have been in the North (from 34% to 43%) and the South West (from 37% to 45%) while the greatest fall in participation was in the East Midlands (from 48% to 44%).

Again, it is necessary to remember the smaller sample sizes involved when examining regional data, and although with the exception of East Anglia, they are not small, the data should be treated with some caution.

Table 2.13: Current/recent learning by standard region: 1990, 1996, 1999 and 2002 compared				
	1990	1996	1999	2002
	All current/recent and/ or informal learners	Proportion which are current/recent learners		
Total sample	39	40	40	42
Greater London	40	44	46	45
South East	40	38	42	44
South West	43	37	37	45
East Anglia	39	43	48	39
East Midlands	37	50	48	44
West Midlands	46	35	34	40
North West	40	35	41	41
Yorkshire/Humberside	40	52	42	41
North	33	45	34	43

NB Percentages are horizontal

Future intentions to learn

Respondents were asked how likely they were to take up learning in the next three years. Table 2.14 compares those who say they are very or fairly likely to learn in the next three years in 1996, 1999 and 2002. There is a slight increase in the proportion who are very or fairly likely to learn, from 38% in 1996 and 1999 to 41% in 2002, although the proportion who say that they are very likely to take up learning remains the same as in 1999 at 22%.

About a half of ABs (52%) and C1s (48%) say that they are likely to take up learning in the future, compared with 38% of C2s and just 29% of DEs. Since 1999, intentions to learn among the upper and middle classes have increased (from 50% to 52% of ABs; and from 46% to 48% of C1s), while among the lower socio-economic classes, attitudes towards learning seem to have hardened, falling from 38% to 34% among C2s and from 29% to 27% among DEs.

Table 2.14: Future intentions to take up learning, by socio-economic class, 1996, 1999 and 2002 compared								
		Base: all respondents = 100%	Very likely	Fairly likely	Total 'likely'	Fairly unlikely	Very unlikely	Total 'unlikely'	Don't know
2002	Total	4896	22	19	41	10	47	57	3
	AB	906	30	22	52	12	35	47	2
	C1	1398	27	21	48	12	37	49	3
	C2	1084	20	18	38	9	51	60	2
	DE	1509	15	15	29	7	60	68	3
1999	Total	5054	22	16	38	12	47	59	3
	AB	914	31	19	50	14	34	48	2
	C1	1398	28	18	46	14	38	52	3
	C2	1,121	18	16	34	14	48	62	3
	DE	1620	14	13	27	9	61	70	3
1996	Total	4673	20	18	38	9	46	55	7
	AB	963	26	20	46	11	37	48	6
	C1	1262	26	19	45	9	40	49	6
	C2	1089	16	18	34	9	50	59	7
	DE	1358	14	14	28	9	54	63	8

NB Percentages are horizontal

Table 2.15 shows that slightly more women (41%) than men (40%) are likely to take up learning in the future. The table also confirms the findings of past surveys that current participation impacts upon future intentions to learn. Seventy-eight per cent of current learners report that they are likely to take up learning in the future, compared with only 13% of those who have not participated since leaving full-time education.

Table 2.15: Future intentions to take up learning, by gender and learning status

	Total	Men	Women	Current learners	Recent learners	Past learners	None since leaving full-time education
Base: all respondents = 100%	4896	2381	2515	1130	943	1039	1747
Very likely	22	21	23	55	28	9	5
Fairly likely	19	18	19	24	32	19	8
Total 'likely'	41	40	41	78	61	28	13
Fairly unlikely	10	10	9	7	12	15	8
Very unlikely	47	47	47	12	24	55	77
Total 'unlikely'	57	57	56	19	36	69	85
Don't know	3	3	2	3	4	3	2

Employment status also influences future intentions to learn. Only one in eight retired people see themselves as future learners, while around a half of those in employment say that they are likely to take up learning in the future. Unemployed adults (54%) see themselves as being most likely to take up learning in the next three years. Since 1999, future intentions to learn have increased across all groups by 3-4% except the retired, where they have increased only slightly from 11% to 12%.

Table 2.16: Future intentions to take up learning, by employment status

	Total	Full-time	Part-time	Unemployed	Not working	Retired
Base: all respondents = 100%	4896	2008	566	187	739	1188
Very likely	22	26	26	27	21	7
Fairly likely	19	24	22	27	21	6
Total 'likely'	41	50	48	54	43	12
Fairly unlikely	10	12	12	13	11	5
Very unlikely	47	35	37	29	44	81
Total 'unlikely'	57	47	49	42	55	86
Don't know	3	3	3	4	2	2

CHAPTER THREE

What people are learning about

This chapter focuses on the detail of what people say they have been learning about either currently or within the last three years.

In 1996, interviewers carried out personal interviews unaided by technology and the four options were offered on a hand-out card. In both 1999 and 2002, the questionnaire was administered using computer-aided personal interviewing (CAPI) offering the respondent four statements to choose from the screen. (If a respondent could not read the screen, the interviewer would read out the options as appropriate.)

In 1996, all current or recent learners were then asked 'What are you learning about/have you most recently learned about?' This was followed by a probe from the interviewer: *by that I include writing skills, reading and basic maths?* People mentioning more than one subject were asked: *What is/was the main subject?* In 1999 and 2002, respondents were simply asked, unprompted, *What subjects are you learning about/have you most recently learnt about?* The probe on basic skills was not used again in subsequent surveys as its effect appeared to have been minimal and a stronger corpus of specific research has since then been built up by the Basic Skills Agency. A further discussion on this point will be found in Volume 2.

This chapter adopts much the same format as that used for the 1999 survey in the interest of comparability and to endeavour to identify real changes. Allowing individuals themselves to describe what they are studying continues to produce an extensive list of subject areas and Table 3.1 adopts the same detailed alphabetical format used in previous reports showing 'all subjects learnt about' in 1996 and 1999, followed by 'all' subjects in 2002, analysed by nations of the UK. The final column provides a total comparison with the main/only subject being studied. While the nations are represented in their correct proportion in the UK population, the sample for Wales was boosted to 995 and is re-weighted for this report. Wales is also the subject of a separate chapter. The sample sizes for Scotland and Northern Ireland, though in their correct proportion, are quite small and should be interpreted with care.

Inevitably, there is a long tail of small subject areas mentioned and many apparently obvious subjects are mentioned by very small numbers. It should be remembered, however, that 1% of current/recent adult learners grosses up to 200,000 individuals in the population as a whole.

The range of subjects listed in Table 3.1 has been kept essentially the same over the three surveys, though they are offered in more usable groupings in later tables. A number of newer subject areas which have been developed are included for 2002, or categories which would include them have been extended and these are identified in the tables. Basic skills, for example, include reading, writing and literacy in the list, preceded by basic maths/numeracy. Added to the list for 2002 were the contemporary subjects of 'communications skills including customer care' and 'self-development/assertiveness training'. More difficult to identify is the area of 'informal and community' learning, as are general 'learning to learn' and other such courses. While the numbers engaged in them at any one time are not great, they form a important route into learning and their role is discussed in more detail in McGivney's chapter in Volume 2.

The chapter by Steve Leman in Volume 2 considers the difference sources of survey evidence in the field. The NALS survey sequence developed, in 1997, a distinction between taught and non-taught courses, and offered detailed prompts about what could be included as learning. The NALS non-taught categories included going to lectures and reading journals, while the taught categories included learning to drive. It is highly unlikely that such activities would have been captured in the NIACE sequence of surveys, and indeed direct comparisons with the NALS survey showed that probing for more detailed responses did indeed elicit more descriptions of shorter episodes particularly of workplace-based learning. The 1996 NIACE survey, on the other hand, produced fewer but longer episodes of learning, more of which were aiming for qualifications. (*The Learning Divide*, 1997)

Patterns of subject choice: 1996, 1999 and 2002 compared

Apart from the ever-increasing impact of computer skills and ICT on the range of learning undertaken, the 2002 study shows a very similar picture to 1999 and 1996. Computer skills rated 17% in 1996, increasing to 25% in 1999 and 29 % in 2002. Between 1996 and 1999, three subject areas appeared to have decreased in take-up: social sciences from 6% to 3%, business/management from 12% to 10% and other professional qualifications from 11% to 7%. Two subjects increased their take-up marginally between 1996 and 1999: nursing/health studies from 8% to 10%, and creative arts from 3% to 5%. The subjects that have decreased somewhat in 2002 are business/management, by 2%, and the proportion studying for professional and vocational qualifications now combined, which has dropped from 18% to 12%. Given the impact of new communications technology on industry in all its forms and the multi-disciplinary nature of many courses, these shifts may well be inter-related.

Health studies and medicine has maintained its level at 10% in 2002 and is now the second highest subject listed leading business studies/management, also at 10%, by a fraction. Creative arts with photography has also maintained its increase at 6% and has just overtaken foreign languages which have continued to decline from its high point of 9% in 1990 and

Table 3.1: All subjects of study, by nations of the UK (in alphabetical order), 1996, 1999 and 2002 compared

| | 1996 | 1999 | | 2002 | | | | |
| | | | UK | Nation | | | | UK |
	All subjects	All subjects	All subjects	England	Wales	Scotland	Northern Ireland	Main subject
Base: all current /recent learners = 100%	1892	2044	2073	1711	94	211	58	2073
Accountancy	4	4	3	4	3	*	4	2
Arts: painting/pottery/ sculpture/design	3	5	5	5	5	6	1	3
Basic skills: reading/writing/ literacy	1	*	1	1	2	1	1	*
Basic maths/numeracy	2	1	1	1	1	1	1	*
Building trades	1	1	1	1	2	1	1	1
Business studies/management including HR and marketing	12	10	8	8	8	6	4	5
Car maintenance	1	1	1	1	1	1	–	*
Carpentry/DIY/handicrafts	3	2	1	1	2	*	–	1
Computer skills/ICT	17	25	29	29	27	27	32	24
Communication skills/ customer care	NSR	NSR	2	2	2	2	1	1
Cookery/catering	3	3	2	2	3	4	3	2
Dance	1	1	1	1	1	1	2	1
Dressmaking/tailoring/needle-work	1	1	1	1	1	–	–	*
Driving (including HGV)	NSR	1	1	1	1	2	10	1
English as a second language/ additional language	1	1	1	1	1	–	–	*
English language/literature	4	4	3	3	3	2	4	1
Engineering	4	4	5	5	4	6	10	4
Foreign languages	8	7	5	5	6	6	8	4
Gardening/horticulture	1	2	2	2	2	2	2	1
History/local history	4	3	4	4	2	2	2	2
Informal/community learning	NSR	NSR	1	1	1	1	2	*
Law	3	2	2	2	2	3	1	2
Mother tongue other than English/Welsh	NSR	NSR	*	*	1	1	–	*

| | 1996 | 1999 | 2002 | | | | | |
| | | | UK | Nation | | | | UK |
	All subjects	All subjects	All subjects	England	Wales	Scotland	Northern Ireland	Main subject
Music	3	2	3	2	4	6	1	1
Nursing/first-aid/health studies	8	10	10	10	7	10	7	6
Photography	1	1	1	1	–	*	–	*
Religion/bible studies/theology	2	2	2	2	1	2	3	1
Science/maths/statistics	4	5	4	5	4	2	6	3
Self development /assertiveness	NSR	NSR	1	1	1	2	3	1
Shorthand/typing/office training	2	1	*	*	1	1	–	*
Social sciences	6	3	4	4	4	4	9	2
Social work/social services/ community care	4	3	3	3	2	4	11	2
Sports/ gymnastics/keep-fit	3	3	2	2	3	3	–	1
Welsh language	NSR	*	*	*	5	–	–	*
Other professional/vocational qualifications	9	9						
Vocational qualification	9	9	12	13	14	12	8	11
Other academic subjects	7	7	8	8	6	8	5	6
Other "leisure" subjects	6	7	6	6	5	7	9	4
Don't know	NSR	NSR	*	*	–	*	–	3

now records only 5%. Some of these movements have undoubtedly been affected by changes in provision, in funding and by the job market. Subsequent sections which look at broader subject groupings against age and employment status help explain some of the changes.

Table 3.2 covers much the same ground as Table 3.1 but concentrates on the 2002 survey and summarises the main groupings of 'all' subjects studied analysed by the four nations but providing a more manageable set of groupings to consider. This offers a clearer picture of the balance between learning which could loosely be described as vocational or non-vocational, a point to be returned to later in relation to age. Computer skills dominate in all the four nations, followed by the grouping of professional and vocational qualifications in all but Northern Ireland. Health studies and medicine come next both in England and Scotland with social sciences/social care higher in Northern Ireland, though the size of the sample is small.

Table 3.2: All subjects of study – summary of main groupings over 2%, by nations of the UK					
	All	England	Wales	Scotland	Northern Ireland
Base: all current/recent learners = 100%	2073	1711	94	211	58
Computer skills/ICT	29	29	27	27	32
Nursing/health studies/medicine/first-aid	10	10	7	10	7
Business studies/management including HR and marketing	8	8	8	6	4
Social sciences/social work/community care	7	7	6	8	19
Creative arts including photography	6	6	5	7	1
Foreign languages	5	5	6	6	8
Engineering (electronic/mechanical/construction)	5	5	4	6	10
Science/maths/statistics	4	5	4	2	6
History/local history	4	4	2	2	2
Accountancy	3	4	3	*	4
English language/literature*	3	3	3	2	4
Music	3	2	4	6	1
Other professional and vocational qualifications	12	13	14	12	8
Other academic subjects	8	8	6	8	5
Other "leisure" subjects	6	6	5	7	9

* An additional 1% specified English as a foreign language or as a second language

Patterns of subject choice in relation to age and employment status

Although lifelong learning as a concept has gained political and social approval, patterns of learning are still affected by habit and expectations as well as funding arrangements. The two decades covered by these surveys have been years in which priority has been given to the young, and to vocational education and much of the generous provision of adult education has been cut back and in some areas closed down completely. While the ACACE proposals for Continuing Education (ACACE, 1982b) received intellectual approval from the then Minister of Education, Keith Joseph, he made it quite clear that adult learning should be personally and privately paid for. The 1991 survey coincided with a subsequent Conservative Government inventing Schedule 2 and classing much general adult education as not appropriate to be funded under the 1992 Act. This, coupled with the cutting back of local authority budgets, has dramatically reduced the availability of local authority provision and hence of affordable and accessible local provision.

While some further education colleges upon being given their independence in 1988 have continued to make proper provision for adult learning, many others have not and have indeed switched resources which used to be available for adults to focus on youth and up-skilling. It is to be hoped that the setting up of the Learning and Skills Council, with its associated local councils and local lifelong learning development plans, heralds an era of more generous provision for adults and allows the rebuilding of adult and community provision and thereby encourages more demand. The difficulty about demand and supply with adults, as the OU, EDAP schemes and adult literacy campaigns have all demonstrated, is that adults are not very good at demanding something that they cannot already see being provided. Many people have simply forgotten that there used to be such provision or that it could or should be set up again.

The difficulty is that the provision wanted and needed by older people is quite different from that needed and wanted by the young. It is obvious that people's interest and desire for learning will vary over their lifecycle and their interest in particular subject areas will vary, as will their own needs. The lifelong learning proposition is not that there is a new and specific tranche or sector of learning provision, but that a wide range of learning opportunities should be available which people can take advantage of easily, without barriers, throughout their lives. The assumption that learning which is vocational or work-related is intrinsically better than learning which may, for example, keep somebody in work or out of hospital is arguable. Both are needed and it is necessary to have rational and equitable ways of funding them both.

Table 3.3 shows some interesting differences in the subjects people choose to learn at different ages. The younger age groups learn computer skills at lower rates than older people now do, presumably because they have already learnt more at school. All adult age groups from 25 onwards are now learning computer skills at a higher rate than three years ago. The proportions studying health/medicine have also increased among all the age groups up to 44 years. Some subjects are clearly studied more by younger age groups, effectively as part of their initial education: business studies, science and maths, creative arts, English, social sciences and other academic subjects. There is encouraging evidence of returning to learning or up-skilling in the middle years with nursing/health studies attracting 12% of 25-44-year-olds and professional and vocational qualifications similarly being chosen by 17% of the 25-44 age group. Significantly more older people are studying computer skills than any other subject: 36% of 55-64-year-olds, 28% of 65-74-year-olds and 23% of those aged 75 and over. Other subjects that specifically attract the older age groups are foreign languages, the creative arts, history and local history and a mixture of other 'leisure' subjects.

For many people, work provides both the incentive to continue learning and the place in which learning may take place or be supported. Table 3.4 analyses all subjects of current/recent study against employment status. It is most interesting to see what subjects are being studied by the unemployed and those working part-time. Thirty-eight per cent of

Table 3.3: All subjects of current/recent study, by age – summary of main groupings over 2%

	All	17-19	20-24	25-34	35-44	45-54	55-64	65-74	75+
Base: all current/recent learners = 100%	2073	194	241	448	494	331	212	115	38
Computer skills/ICT	29	19	15	27	33	37	36	28	23
Nursing/health studies/medicine/ first-aid	10	10	7	12	12	9	8	2	5
Business studies/management including HR and marketing	8	13	15	8	6	6	4	1	–
Creative arts including photography	6	11	3	4	3	4	9	19	15
Foreign languages	5	2	3	4	4	7	9	10	15
Engineering (electronic/mechanical/ construction)	5	5	6	7	4	4	3	1	3
Social sciences	4	9	9	2	5	3	2	1	8
Science/maths/statistics	4	14	9	3	2	3	1	2	–
History/local history	4	6	3	1	1	5	7	8	14
Accountancy	3	3	5	4	4	1	2	1	–
Social work/social services/ community care	3	1	2	4	4	4	2	1	2
English language/literature*	3	10	4	3	2	1	1	*	2
Music	3	3	1	3	2	3	3	6	6
Other professional and vocational qualifications	12	12	10	17	17	10	5	5	2
Other academic subjects	8	18	12	6	6	7	5	6	7
Other "leisure" subjects	6	5	5	3	4	5	12	12	8

* An additional 1% specified English as a foreign language or as a second language

Figure 3.1 Current/recent study of the top five subject areas, by age

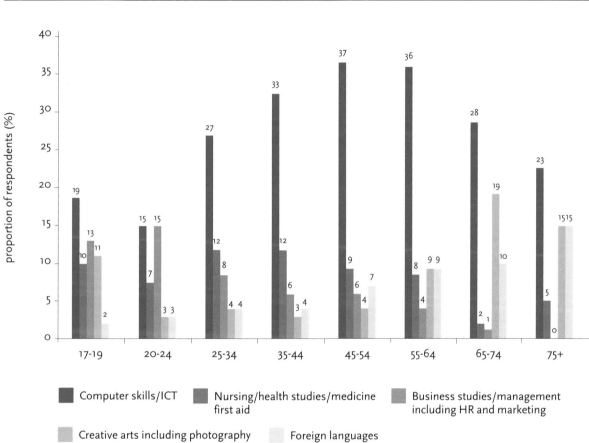

the unemployed and 33% of those who are not working are studying computer skills, compared with 29% overall. Encouragingly, 12% of both those working full-time and part-time are studying nursing/health studies. Ten per cent of the unemployed are studying engineering, and 4% are studying social sciences. Of course, more people are now in full-time employment and therefore the availability of employer support, particularly time off for study, becomes important. Sixteen per cent of those working full-time and 12% of those working part-time are choosing to study for professional or vocational qualifications.

Full-time students, usually completing their initial education, are studying a broader range of subjects than those studying part-time: a smaller group (15%) are concentrating on computer skills; 13% are studying science, maths or statistics; 12% business studies/management; 9% English language/literature; 10% creative arts; 10% social sciences; 9% nursing/health studies; and 17% are studying a range of other academic subjects.

Figure 3.2 Key areas of current/recent study, by employment status

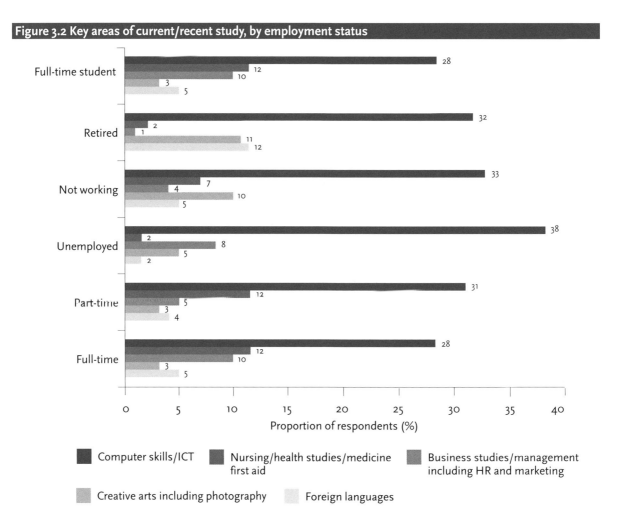

Computer skills/ICT   Nursing/health studies/medicine   Business studies/management
                       first aid   including HR and marketing

Creative arts including photography   Foreign languages

Table 3.4: All subjects of current/recent study, by employment status – summary of main groupings over 2%						
	All	Full-time	Part-time	Unemployed	Not working	Retired	Student
Base: all current/recent learners = 100%	2073	1041	290	86	226	225	201
Computer skills/ICT	29	28	31	38	33	32	15
Nursing/health studies/medicine/ first-aid	10	12	12	2	7	2	9
Business studies/ management including HR and marketing	8	10	5	8	4	–	12
Creative arts including photography	6	3	3	5	10	15	10
Foreign languages	5	5	4	2	5	12	3
Engineering (electronic/mechanical/ construction)	5	7	2	10	1	1	7
Social sciences	4	3	8	4	6	2	10
Science/maths/statistics	4	3	4	4	5	1	13
History/local history	4	2	3	–	3	11	6
Accountancy	3	4	3	5	1	1	3
Social work/social services/ community care	3	3	5	2	5	1	1
English language/literature*	3	2	4	3	4	1	9
Music	3	3	1	1	3	6	2
Other professional and vocational qualifications	12	16	12	9	9	4	8
Other academic subjects	8	7	8	7	8	6	17
Other "leisure" subjects	6	3	5	9	10	15	5

* An additional 1% specified English as a foreign language or as a second language

Main or only subjects of study, by gender: 1996, 1999 and 2002 compared

Many adults are or have been currently or recently learning about more than one subject and this chapter has so far attempted to provide an overview of all these subjects. It is unrealistic in such a survey to ask more detailed questions about location, provider *etc* for every subject studied, and learners who are studying more than one subject are therefore asked to identify their main subject. The next sequence of tables focus down on the 'main' or 'only' subject being studied and offers a different perspective of the subject balance over the years, particularly in relation to differences between men and women. The general picture of the increase in computer studies/ICT appearing to overtake in popularity a wide range of other business, professional and vocational areas continues to hold (Table 3.5). The remainder of the smaller subjects all maintain their positions, but with a small cumulative decrease in the 'leisure' and softer subject areas. Nursing/health studies still holds a high position among women, but has slipped three per cent from 1999. It is encouraging that engineering has maintained its rating at 4% from 1999 and that science and maths has moved in the right direction, up to 3%. (Subjects new to the survey have not been included in this table unless they rank over 1%.)

Table 3.5: Main or only subject of current/recent study, by gender, 1996, 1999 and 2002 compared								
	2002			1999			1996		
	All	Men	Women	All	Men	Women	All	Men	Women
Base: all current/recent learners = 100%	2073	1015	1059	2044	980	1064	1812	982	910
Computer skills/ICT	24	26	22	19	21	17	12	13	11
Other professional and vocational qualifications	11	10	12	16	17	15	18	18	18
Other academic subjects	6	5	7	8	8	8	4	4	4
Nursing/health studies/medicine/ first-aid	6	4	9	7	2	12	6	3	9
Business studies/management including HR and marketing	5	6	4	7	8	5	9	11	8
Other "leisure" subjects	4	4	5	6	5	7	4	4	4
Foreign languages excluding Welsh	4	4	4	4	4	4	5	6	5
Engineering (electronic/mechanical/ construction)	4	7	*	4	8	–	3	6	1
Arts: painting/pottery/design/ photography/ sculpture	3	2	4	3	3	4	2	1	3
Science/maths/statistics	3	3	2	2	2	2	3	4	2
Accountancy	2	3	2	2	2	2	2	2	2
Social sciences	2	2	3	1	1	2	4	4	5
Social work/community care	2	1	4	2	1	3	3	2	5
History/local history	2	2	2	2	2	1	2	2	2
Law/bar exams	2	2	1	1	2	1	2	2	1
Cookery/catering	2	1	2	2	1	2	3	2	3
English language/literature*	2	1	2	2	1	3	2	1	2
Music	1	2	1	2	2	1	2	2	2
Handicrafts/DIY	1	1	*	1	1	1	2	2	1

* subjects over 1% only listed

Figure 3.3: The top six main or only subject of current/recent study, by gender, 2002

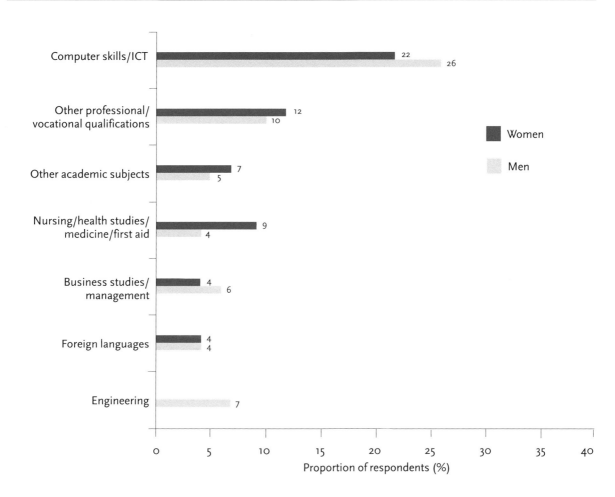

Table 3.6 analyses main or only subject of study against reasons for study, and against whether or not people are aiming for a qualification. In previous surveys, respondents have been asked to give their *main* reason for studying their main (or only) subject, and this has provided a fairly clear differentiation between the three main motivational groups: work-related study, study for education/progression and study for personal development. Given the opportunity in 2002, a large number of respondents have offered more than one reason for studying their main/only subject and they have therefore been included in more than one column as appropriate. These overlapping motivational issues are looked at in more detail in Chapter 6. While computer studies/ICT ranks highest as a work-related reason (26%), it also ranks as high among those studying for personal development (25%) and nearly as high among those studying for education/progression (21%). Nursing/health studies is an interesting exampled of an area that ranks highest against education/progression (9%) and also records 7% as work-related, with 8% aiming for a qualification. It also attracts across more mature learners, recording 12% among both 25-34-year-olds and 35-44-year-olds.

While the majority of learners overall are aiming for a qualification, significantly more learners studying computing (30%) are not aiming for a qualification than those who are (20%)!

A group of increasing interest are those people who say that their subject of study is not their choice (Table 3.6). The proportion saying this has increased from 4% in 1999 to 6% in 2002. Apart from the obvious need in many jobs to become computer-literate (25% whose choice was not their own are studying ICT), professional and vocational areas (mentioned by 26%) now have compulsory updating requirements and there are also national requirements for

Table 3.6: Main or only subject of current/recent study, by gender, reasons for study and whether a qualification was aimed for

		Gender			Reasons for study			Qualification	
	All	Men	Women	Work related	Education/ progression	Personal development	Not my choice	Aimed for	Not aimed for
Base: all current/ recent learners =100%	2073	1015	1059	1105	564	1295	134	1258	704
Computer skills/ICT	24	26	22	26	21	25	25	20	30
Other professional and vocational qualifications	11	10	12	14	13	8	26	13	7
Other academic subjects	6	5	7	7	8	6	5	8	4
Nursing/health studies/ medicine/first-aid	6	4	9	7	9	4	6	8	4
Business studies/management including HR and marketing	5	6	4	7	8	4	4	6	3
Other "leisure" subjects	4	4	5	2	2	6	4	2	8
Foreign languages excluding Welsh	4	4	4	1	1	5	1	2	8
Engineering (electronic/ mechanical/construction)	4	7	*	4	5	3	5	5	2
Arts: painting/pottery/design/ photography/ sculpture	3	2	5	1	2	5	–	2	6
Science/maths/ statistics	3	3	2	3	5	3	4	4	1
Accountancy	2	3	2	3	4	2	3	3	1
Social sciences	2	2	3	2	4	3	1	3	1
Social work/ community care	2	1	4	3	3	2	1	3	2
History/local history	2	2	2	*	1	3	–	1	3
Law/bar exams	2	2	1	2	3	1	2	3	1
Cookery/catering	2	1	2	2	1	1	4	2	2
English language/literature*	1	1	2	1	1	2	–	2	1
Don't know which	3	3	3	3	2	2	3	3	3

* Includes ESOL, at less than 0.5%

health and safety training etc. Concern has been expressed elsewhere that the increase of compulsory updating/life-long learning may be damaging to an individual's other learning needs and motivation.

A more general concern has been that the emphasis nationally has been on skills and accredited work-related or vocational training for so long that the wider lifelong-learning provision has withered and even died away in some areas. The current dominance of computer studies now adds to this concern as until ICT needs are regularly met or built into content-led programmes, other subject areas are going to find it hard to survive and attract an appropriate number of learners. A similar issue is the difficulty of re-building recruitment and training in large areas of the public sector, after many years of cut-back or neglect.

Reasons for choosing the main/only subject of current/recent study, by gender and age

Allowing people to offer more than one reason for their main subject of study has encouraged a wider variety of reasons to be given and is helpful in reminding us that many people have a mix of motives for study. A recent study along similar lines carried out in Great Britain by NIACE with partners in Norway and Spain (Skaalvik and Finbak, *Adult Education in Great Britain, Norway and Spain*, 2001) carried out a regression analysis on a set of similar attitudes/variables and suggested that, in Norway and Spain, there were only two main groups where studying for a qualification clustered with work-related motives. Table 3.7 includes the total column from 1999 to offer a feel of how the pattern of answers has increased, and whether it appears to have fundamentally changed the balance of intentions. 'Gaining a recognised qualification' has risen from 9% to 24%, with education/progression together increasing from 11% to 27%. Personal development as a group has nearly doubled from 35% to 62%, while the groupings of work-related reasons has only increased from 47% to 53%.

The increase in 'personal development' may well be due to an additional reason in the 2002 survey: 'to improve my self-confidence'. This motive was responsible for 12% overall, rising to 14% among all those aged between 25 and 54, the bulk of mature learners. A second new option was included, relating to the understanding of 'informal learning', 'as a result of participating in another activity' and this produced a modest 3%, rising to 6% among 55-64-year-olds and 4% among people 65 and over. An interesting question to consider is whether the intention to learn is present before undertaking the activity or whether the learning is recognised as such after the activity is ended.

The general pattern of reasons given for studying people's main/only subject of study is surprisingly gender-free particularly in relation to work-related motives (Table 3.7). Somewhat more men than women (by 5%) mention 'wanting help in my current job' and 'to gain a rise in earnings' (by 3%). More women than men (15% compared to 6%) want to improve their

Table 3.7: Reasons for choosing subject of main learning, by gender and age

	All	Men	Women	17-19	20-24	25-34	35-44	45-54	55-64	65-74	75+	1999 total
Base: all current/ recent learners = 100%	2073	1015	1059	194	241	448	494	331	212	115	38	2044
Interested in the subject	34	33	34	39	39	28	27	33	42	47	49	23
To develop myself as a person	25	24	25	20	24	26	30	25	17	18	21	8
I enjoy learning	31	29	33	32	30	27	26	28	43	47	61	4
To meet people	8	7	8	9	14	7	5	6	9	11	11	1
To improve my self-confidence	12	9	15	8	10	14	14	14	11	9	5	NA
All giving personal development reasons	62	61	64	63	67	57	56	62	71	80	88	35
To get a recognised qualification	24	24	24	40	39	31	23	15	9	2	2	9
To help me get on a future course	6	5	7	16	11	7	6	2	2	1	3	2
All giving education/ progression reasons	27	26	28	48	46	34	25	16	12	3	5	11
To get a job	17	17	17	44	40	21	9	7	3	2	–	10
To help me in my current job	26	28	23	7	14	30	37	35	20	6	2	17
To change the type of work I do	8	9	7	2	7	15	10	5	3	1	3	4
To gain a promotion	7	8	6	3	8	12	8	7	1	–	–	5
To make my work more satisfying	13	14	12	7	12	17	14	14	9	4	5	4
To gain a rise in earnings	8	9	6	4	15	14	7	4	2	–	–	2
To get a job with a different employer	5	5	5	2	7	8	6	6	1	1	–	1
Had no choice – employer requirement	4	5	4	*	2	5	7	5	6	2		3
Had no choice – professional requirement	2	2	1	1	*	3	3	2	–	2	–	1
All giving work-related reasons	53	56	51	56	65	66	58	52	31	12	8	47
As a result of participating in another activity	3	2	3	2	1	2	2	3	6	4	4	NA

self-confidence. Age is a much clearer discriminator than gender in relation to people's motives for learning. Forty per cent of younger people up to 25 mention the need to get a recognised qualification as do 31% of 25-34-year-olds and 23% of 35-44-year-olds. The two youngest age-groups are similarly most keen to get a job. Intrinsic interest remains important both for the younger age-groups and the older groups, while people in their middle years tend to emphasise work-related reasons, 'to help in their current job', 'to gain a rise in earnings' or 'to make their work more satisfying'. 'I enjoy learning/gives me pleasure' is the other main reason among the older age groups.

Subjects named for future learning

Chapter 2 discussed in some detail respondent's future intentions to learn in the future. The proportion that were 'very' or 'fairly' likely to learn within the next three years remained stable between 1996 and 1999 at 38%. There is an encouraging increase of 3% overall in 2002, with an increase of 4% among the skilled working class (C2). However, the increases are mainly among those who are 'fairly likely' to learn rather than those who are 'very likely to'.

All respondents, irrespective of whether or not they 'indicated' any future intentions to learn, were asked:

> "What (else), if anything, would you be interested in learning about if you could?"

Following the practice of the previous surveys, respondents were not prompted in any way, but the answers they gave are categorised according to the same headings and subject areas as in the earlier questions.

Table 3.8 shows the overall proportion of respondents in different socio-economic and demographic groups who do, in fact, offer a subject/area of learning comparing 1996,1999 and 2002. The proportion who do so has dropped gradually from 69% in 1996 to 62% in 2002, though with no difference between men and women. The vast majority of younger people name subjects they plan to study: 77-78% of all those aged 17-34. The proportions then decline steadily as people get older.

There is a similar decline shown by socio-economic class, with 73% of AB's naming subjects, followed by 68% of C1s, 63% of C2s and 51% of DEs. This mirrors closely the drop between current, recent, past and non-learners from 76% to 46%.

The concern is that while the young, current learners and the upper class are definite about their choices, other groups are less so.

Table 3.8: Proportion of groups specified giving subjects they would like to learn about: 1996, 1999 and 2002 compared

	2002	1999	1996
All respondents	62	66	69
Gender			
Male	63	67	69
Female	62	65	69
Age			
17-19	78	77	74
20-24	77	81	80
25-34	77	78	77
35-44	68	75	76
45-54	63	68	71
55-64	56	58	63
65-74	43	47	57
75 and over	30	30	46
Socio-economic group			
AB	73	74	74
C1	68	70	72
C2	63	68	67
DE	51	55	65
Learning status			
Current learning	76	78	77
Recent learning	74	78	80
Past learning	66	70	74
None since leaving full-time education	46	51	56

Percentages are horizontal

Table 3.9 focuses only on those who name subjects they are interested in learning about and compares subject of interest to men and women in 1999 and 2002. Computer studies continues to increase its hold on the market with 28% overall, and 31% of men and 25% of women, choosing it. The next highest subject continues to be foreign languages (12%) well ahead of any other subject areas.

Table 3.9: Subjects people are interested in learning about in the future, 1999 and 2002 compared, based on all giving subjects (2% or over listed)

	2002			1999		
	All	Men	Women	All	Men	Women
Base: all giving subjects = 100%	3058	1494	1564	3319	1580	1739
Computer studies	28	31	25	24	27	20
Foreign languages	12	12	11	13	14	12
Creative arts: painting, sculpture, pottery	7	5	9	6	4	8
Social sciences/services, social work, community care	6	3	9	5	3	7
History/local history	6	7	5	5	5	5
Other professional and vocational qualifications	5	3	7	7	7	7
Nursing, health studies, first aid, medicine	5	2	7	5	1	9
Handicrafts/carpentry/DIY*	4	6	3	4	4	5
Gardening/flower-arranging/ horticulture	4	4	5	4	3	4
Music, learning an instrument, singing	4	5	3	3	4	2
Cookery/catering	4	2	6	4	2	6
Business/administration/management	4	5	2	5	5	5
Engineering	3	6	*	3	6	*
Physical sports/keep-fit	3	4	1	2	3	2
Accountancy	3	3	3	3	2	3
Mathematics/science	3	3	2	2	2	1
Driving (inc. HGV)	2	3	2	1	1	1
Car maintenance	2	4	1	2	4	1
Photography	2	4	1	2	3	1
Law/bar exams	2	2	2	2	2	2
Dressmaking/needlecrafts	2	*	4	2	*	4
English language/literature	2	2	2	3	2	4
Other 'leisure' subjects	5	4	6	9	9	9
Other academic subjects	3	3	3	3	4	3

*DIY/handicrafts/carpentry were merged in 2002.

There are some areas where there are differences between men and women and mainly these are work-related: 9% of women mention social science and social work, and 7% of women mention professional and vocational qualifications and also nursing/health studies. More men mention engineering (6%) and handicrafts/DIY (6%) and business/management (5%). Other male preferences include car maintenance (4%), sports (4%), and building trades (3%). An area that has increased its share gradually over the years is the arts, including painting, writing, photography *etc* (7%).

Table 3.10 covers the same set of subject areas, but includes the responses for the whole range of the adult population irrespective of whether or not they have definite plans about learning in the next three years. The challenge is however, of course, to reach those who are not currently interested.

The range of subjects is again extremely broad and the table includes only subjects gaining 2% or more mentions. It is worth noting that 1% of current/recent learners represents 200,000 people so these subjects potentially represent sizeable groups of people. Examples of such small subjects registering 1% or less are basic maths (23 mentions), English as a second language (21 mentions), basic skills (17 mentions), other mother tongue languages (15 mentions) and Welsh (13 mentions). The key groups of people who are of most immediate interest as continuing or future learners, are current learners and those likely to learn in the next three years.

Among future learners one quarter mention computer studies, 9% foreign languages and 9% creative arts. Table 3.11 summarises these main groups in a more digestable way.

Table 3.10: Subjects people are interested in learning about in the future, by learning status and future learning intentions – all adults							
		Learning status				Future learning in next three years	
	Total	Current learners	Recent learners	Past learners	None since full-time education	Likely	Unlikely
Base: all respondents = 100%	4869	1130	943	1039	1747	1986	2777
Computer studies	17	15	19	23	14	24	13
Foreign languages	7	10	8	9	4	9	6
Arts: painting/pottery/sculpture/ photography	6	9	7	6	3	9	4
History/local history	4	3	4	5	3	4	4
Nursing/health studies/medicine	3	4	4	2	2	5	1
Handicrafts/DIY/carpentry	3	2	3	3	3	3	3
Gardening	3	2	2	3	3	2	3
Music	3	5	3	2	1	4	2
Cookery/catering	2	2	3	2	3	3	2
Business/administration/ management	2	3	3	3	1	4	1
Engineering	2	3	3	2	1	3	1
Social sciences	2	5	2	1	*	4	1
Social work/services/care	2	2	2	2	2	3	1
Sports/keep-fit	2	3	2	2	1	2	2
Accountancy	2	3	2	2	1	3	1
Mathematics/science	2	4	2	1	1	3	1
Driving including HGV	2	2	2	1	2	2	1
English language/literature	1	2	1	1	1	2	1
Other professional and vocational qualifications	3	5	5	3	2	6	1
Other leisure subjects	3	3	4	4	1	4	3
Other academic subjects	2	3	3	1	1	3	1
All naming subjects	62	76	74	66	46	84	47
None/nothing	38	24	26	34	54	16	53

Table 3.11: Main subjects of future interest to current learners and future learners

	Total	Current learners	Future learning in next 3 years
Base: all respondents = 100%	4896	1130	1986
Computer studies	17	15	24
Foreign languages	7	10	9
Creative arts	6	9	9
Nursing/health studies	3	4	5
Business/administration/management	2	3	4
History/local history	4	3	4
Other professional and vocational qualifications	3	5	6
Other leisure subjects	3	3	4

Table 3.12 focusses on the main subjects of interest to older learners. While computer studies maintains its position at the top of the list, followed at a distance by foreign languages, the array of subjects of interest to older people is much wider and includes many subjects that were typically provided through 'adult education' in its more generously-provided-for days. Examples are the creative arts, cookery, and DIY/carpentry. It will be important to ensure that some of this provision is reinstated and offered in accessible ways if older people are to be attracted back into learning.

Table 3.12: Main subject of interest to older learners

	55-64	65-74	75+
Base: all respondents = 100%	705	583	375
Computer studies/ICT	17	11	6
Foreign languages	8	6	4
Arts: including painting/writing/photography	6	7	3
History/local history	5	3	4
Gardening/floristry	5	4	3
DIY/carpentry/handicrafts	3	2	2
Cookery/catering	3	2	2
Dressmaking/needlecrafts	2	2	2
Other leisure subjects	3	3	3

CHAPTER FOUR

Source of information about learning, its location and length

Adults find out about learning opportunities in a variety of ways and from a variety of sources. Issues about the provision of information, advice and guidance become more important as people enter and re-enter learning opportunities at different stages in their lives. Useful sources of information for the young are not necessarily useful for older people. Some providers are beginning to use new communications technologies both for information and course delivery, but many existing and potential learners do not yet have appropriate access to PCs and the internet, an issue looked at further in Chapter 8. While the internet will play an increasingly important role in the provision of advice and guidance, its use is developing less fast than some people hoped and assumed. What has been established over the past decade is the value of telephone helplines and it is significant that the University for Industry has re-branded itself as 'learndirect' essentially taking over the function of the telephone helpline 'Learning Direct' and integrating it into the UfI's services. The learndirect helpline received 1.3 million calls during the 2001/02 financial year.

The workplace continues to dominate as the main source of information about learning (Table 4.1). The survey question distinguishes between those who answer 'work: my employer/personnel/training officer' (down to 20% from 25% in 1999) and those who mention their workmates/colleagues (up from 7% to 12% in 2002). There are no other significant changes between 1999 and 2002. Friends/family takes over in second place, mentioned by 13%, followed by workmates (12%) and further education at 11%. Others, all ranked at 7%, are newspapers/magazines, university/other HE, and school. Adult education centres/WEA now rank at 4%. Table 4.1 lists all categories over 1%, but there is a long tail of new categories which were included on the questionnaire this time, but do not yet rank over 1%. These include the internet/web reaching 1%, TV/radio (24 mentions), learndirect (14 mentions) social/outreach worker (11 mentions), GP (6 mentions) and health club (4 mentions).

University/HE is less important as a source of information in Scotland and Northern Ireland, as is further education. Northern Ireland prefers less formal routes such as friends/family, the local school or workmates. In Wales, the further education system ranks higher in comparison.

Table 4.1: Source of information about main current/recent learning*, by nation of the UK						
		2002				1999
	UK	England	Wales	Scotland	Northern Ireland	
Base: all current/recent learners = 100%	2073	1711	94	211	58	2044
Work/employer/training officer	20	21	20	17	20	25
Friends/family	13	13	15	14	34	12
Work-mates	12	12	7	14	16	7
Further education college/technical college	11	11	14	9	4	13
University/college of higher education/OU	7	7	7	3	4	8
School	7	7	6	8	12	6
Newspaper/magazines	7	7	6	13	7	6
Adult education centre including WEA	4	4	4	*	1	3
Printed publicity delivered to home	3	3	4	1	9	3
Printed publicity elsewhere	2	2	4	2	3	3
Library	2	2	2	3	2	2
Job centre/job club/employment service e.g. New Deal	2	2	2	3	–	2
Careers/guidance service	2	2	3	2	–	2
Internet/www	2	2	2	2	1	1
Community centre/voluntary organisation/religious group	2	1	1	3	4	1
Trade union/professional association	1	1	1	1	2	2

* Sources over 1% only listed.

Table 4.2 compares sources of information for men and women, as well as across the age groups. More men than women, (by 5%) quote work: their employer/personnel or training officer or their workmates (by 2%). Other differences between men and women are not great: 3% more women quote both family/friends and school as a source.

The workplace and workmates dominate all the age groups from 25 to 64. The careers service, now re-establishing itself as Connexions, is only reported by 5% by the two youngest age groups. Among 17-19-year-olds, schools and further education colleges continue to be the main source of information. These are joined by universities among the 20-24-year-olds. Adult education centres/evening institutes increase in importance among middle and older age groups, peaking at 8% among 55-64-year-olds. Community centres/voluntary organisations are also important for older people, with 5% of 65-74s and 8% of 75+ mentioning them.

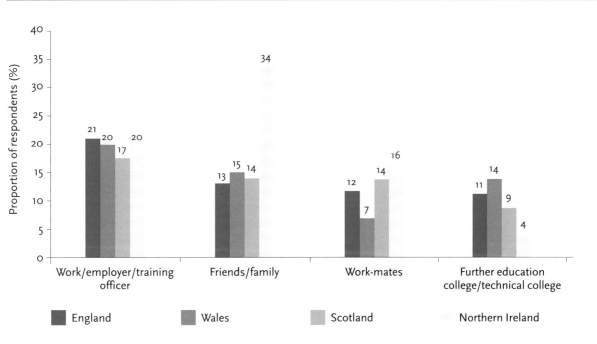

Figure 4.1 Top four sources of information about current/recent learning, by nations of the UK

Newspapers/magazines continue to play an important role particularly for people aged 45 and over; 13% of 45-54s mention them. A further 7% refer to other forms of printed material. It is important that the existing sources of information like print are not closed down before newer ICT-based ones are in place. Libraries, in particular, are developing new ICT-based access and learning roles alongside their original ones. The internet still has a long way to go before it overtakes print and the telephone.

The proportion mentioning the internet has increased but only by 1%, to 2%. At the younger end, 4% of 20-24-year-olds mention the internet as their source of information, as do 4% of men compared with 1% of women. What people use the internet for is considered in more detail in Chapter 8, as is the general issue of access to ICT and the information divide.

Table 4.2: Source of information about main current/recent learning*, by gender and age

	All	Men	Women	17-19	20-24	25-34	35-44	45-54	55-64	65-74	75+
Base: all current/recent learners = 100%	2073	1015	1059	194	241	448	494	331	212	115	38
Work/employer/training officer	20	23	18	5	9	24	29	27	21	4	2
Friends/family	13	12	15	15	22	12	11	9	13	16	28
Work-mates	12	13	11	4	5	16	18	11	10	5	6
Further education college/technical college	11	10	11	27	18	11	7	6	4	9	11
University/college of higher education	7	8	6	8	22	7	4	3	3	2	6
School	7	5	8	29	20	3	2	2	2	3	2
Newspaper/magazines	7	7	8	1	4	6	7	13	11	12	4
Adult education centre including WEA	4	3	4	*	*	2	4	5	8	7	4
Printed publicity delivered to home	3	2	4	1	1	3	3	4	3	4	1
Printed publicity elsewhere	2	2	3	1	2	2	2	3	4	2	4
Library	2	2	2	*	–	2	2	3	3	2	7
Job centre/job club/ employment service e.g. New Deal	2	3	1	3	1	3	1	2	2	–	–
Careers/guidance service/Connexions	2	1	2	5	5	2	1	–	–	–	–
Internet/www	2	4	1	1	4	3	3	2	2	1	–
Community centre/voluntary organisation/religious group	2	1	3	–	–	2	1	2	2	5	8
Trade union/professional association	1	1	*	–	1	1	1	1	1	1	–

* Sources over 1% only listed.

Table 4.3 focuses on sources of information in relation to employment status, qualification aims and future plans for learning. The workplace is most important for those in work, particularly if they are not aiming for a qualification. Further and higher education and schools are most important for those aiming for a qualification, while friends/family and newspapers/magazines are most important for those not aiming for qualifications. There is little difference in sources of information between those who plan to learn in the future and those who do not.

Table 4.3: Source of information about main current/recent learning*, by employment status, whether a qualification is aimed for and future learning intentions

	All	Employment Status						Qualifications		Future learning	
		Full-time	Part-time	Unemployed	Not working	Retired	Full-time student	Aimed for	Not aimed for	Likely	Not likely
Base: all current/ recent learners = 100%	2073	1041	290	86	226	225	201	1258	704	1459	549
Work/employer/training officer	20	32	20	4	4	6	*	18	24	20	20
Friends/family	13	10	15	17	20	18	17	11	18	14	13
Work-mates/ colleagues	12	18	15	1	2	2	2	12	11	12	13
Further education college/ technical college/tertiary/ 6th form	11	7	12	11	13	8	24	15	5	11	9
Newspaper/magazines	7	6	7	7	11	13	3	7	8	7	8
University/ college of higher education	7	6	4	4	3	3	28	11	1	7	5
School	7	3	7	7	6	3	29	10	3	7	7
Adult education centre including WEA	4	2	5	5	5	8	*	3	5	4	3
Printed publicity delivered to home	3	2	4	4	4	3	1	2	3	3	3
Internet/www	2	3	1	2	2	1	3	2	3	3	1
Printed publicity elsewhere	2	2	3	–	5	3	2	2	3	3	1
Library	2	1	2	1	5	4	–	2	3	2	2
Job centre/job club/ employment service e.g. New Deal	2	1	*	21	5	–	1	2	1	2	2
Community centre/voluntary organisation/religious group	2	1	1	–	5	4	1	1	3	1	2
Careers/guidance service/ connexions	2	1	2	4	1	–	5	3	*	2	2
Trade union/professional association	1	1	*	*	–	*	1	1	*	1	1

* Sources over 1% only listed.

The location of people's learning

With the widening of lifelong learning opportunities and the additional choices offered by open and distance learning and new technologies, people are in a position to choose where and how they want to learn. It is no longer necessary to sit in a class-room at a specific time, and the conventional barriers to access of time and place are no longer dominant. The Open University now has over 200,000 graduates, the Open Learning Foundation provides materials across 30 universities and higher education institutions, the National Extension College and the Open College of the Arts extend ODL opportunities across such diverse areas as childcare and creative arts. The most recent arrival is learndirect, soon to be followed by the NHS University. For those in work, the workplace becomes an increasingly important location, both for work-related learning and for more general learning opportunities. These workplace-based trends are likely to be supported by such developments as the Union Learning Fund and Learning Representatives. The survey question has therefore continued

Table 4.4: Main location of current/recent learning, by gender, 1999 and 2002 compared

	All	2002 Men	Women	1999 All
Base: all respondents = 100%	2073	1015	1059	2044
Further education college/ tertiary college/6th form college	21	21	21	20
University/college of higher education/Open University	16	17	15	18
Where I work	15	18	12	18
Adult education centre/evening institute/WEA	7	5	9	8
Private training centre/hotel/conference centre	4	5	3	5
Employer's training centre	5	5	5	5
School	4	3	5	3
Voluntary organisation/informal group, including trade union, WI, WEA, church	3	3	3	2
Local ICT learning centre, e.g. Learndirect, UK On-line	2	1	2	NA
Skills centre/job centre/club	1	*	*	1
At home: informal learning/from book	6	8	5	10
At home: structured correspondence/open learning	3	3	3	2
At home: using a computer, CD ROM, internet	6	7	5	1
At home: from TV/radio	*	*	1	1
Other educational institution	2	1	2	1
Other locations	3	4	2	4

to focus on the location of learning and within that on the type of institution or type of learning, rather than categorising the actual providers of the content or the software used.

Table 4.4 offers an extensive list of locations comparing 1999 with 2002, and men with women. The findings show basic stability between the two surveys. Further education colleges continue to head the list both for men and women. Six per cent more men than women learn in the workplace, while more women learn in adult education centres, by 4%, and in community/leisure centres, by 3%.

Further education colleges are the main place of learning for 17-19-year-olds (49%), 20-24-year-olds (22%) and now also 25-34-year-olds (21%). Universities are the dominant location for 50% of 20-24-year-olds. Further education colleges continue to be an important provider across all the age groups (Table 4.5).

Table 4.5: Main location of current/recent learning, by age, 1999 and 2002 compared										
	All	17-19	20-24	25-34	35-44	45-54	55-64	65-74	75+	1999 All
Base: all respondents = 100%	2073	194	241	448	494	331	212	115	38	2044
Further education college/tertiary college/6th form college	21	49	22	21	17	17	13	15	12	20
University/college of higher education/Open University	16	19	50	17	9	6	11	3	7	18
Where I work	15	8	9	19	19	19	12	2	5	18
Adult education centre/evening institute/WEA	7	2	2	7	8	6	11	17	9	8
Employer's training centre	5	*	2	5	6	7	7	2	–	5
School	4	9	1	3	4	5	3	5	7	3
Community centre/leisure centre	3	1	*	2	2	2	6	8	13	3
Local ICT learning centre, e.g. Learndirect, UK On-line	2	1	1	1	3	1	2	2	3	NA
Voluntary organisation/informal group, e.g. U3A	2	–	–	2	2	1	2	6	2	1
Other educational institution	2	3	1	1	2	2	1	2	–	1
At home: informal learning	6	1	3	4	7	7	10	14	17	10
At home: using a computer, CD ROM, internet	6	1	1	6	7	10	11	5	1	1
At home: structured correspondence/ open learning	3	*	2	4	4	4	1	1	3	1
Other locations	3	1	2	2	2	4	5	6	5	4

The proportion learning at home is also stable between 1999 and 2002 at 14-15%, though fewer (6%) say they are learning informally/from a book, countering more (6%) who are using a computer/CD-ROM or the internet, rising to 11% among 45-64-year-olds. Three per cent specify a structured correspondence course or open learning. The new ICT-equipped local learning centres (e.g. learndirect/UK online) register an encouraging 2%, with 3% among 35-44s. Libraries have dropped to 1% and job centres have dropped to less than 0.5% so neither are shown on the table. An extended list of locations was included in 2002, some of which do not which produce 1% of mentions, but may act as a bench-mark for future developments: e.g. health clubs with 14 mentions and while driving/travelling with four mentions.

Widening participation continues to be a main policy preoccupation, and the Government is now working to a goal of 50% of young people by 2010 having progressed to higher education by the age of 30. To achieve this goal will certainly involve reaching more people in the C1 and C2 socio-economic classes, and ideally also some of those in Group D, unskilled manual workers. Table 4.6 shows location of learning by socio-economic class, urban or rural area and also by groups of reasons for learning. Further education colleges are in the front line for reaching socio-economic groups C2 and DE with 24% of C2s and 31% of DEs studying at them. The largest proportion of C1s (22%) are at university/HE, followed by 18% in further education college. The workplace plays a vital role in reaching skilled manual workers (C2s), 19% of whom are learning in the workplace.

In general, there are fewer differences in participation between urban and rural areas than might have been expected. However, further education colleges rank 4% higher for rural learners than for those in urban areas and the work place is also 3% higher in rural areas. It is universities that pick up an extra 5% in urban areas.

Length of current/recent study

The NIACE surveys, as discussed earlier, ask respondents to describe what they are/were learning in terms of a broadly drafted question, but without the additional prompting and differentiation which has been more recently developed by the NALS survey. The NALS sequence of related prompt questions identifies a much larger number of shorter episodes, particularly of workplace based education and training, many lasting less than one week, while the NIACE surveys pick up proportionately more episodes of longer learning. The 2002 survey shows little change from 1999, but it is worth noting that 2% more women than men are quoting learning episodes of less than three months and 6% fewer women than men are studying for over two years. (Table 4.7)

Table 4.6: Main location of current/recent learning, by socio-economic group, reasons for learning and type of area

	All	AB	C1	C2	DE	Work-related	Education/ progression	Personal development	Rural	Urban
Base: all respondents = 100%	2073	541	759	397	376	1105	564	1295	368	1705
Further education college/tertiary college/6th form college	21	15	18	24	31	21	27	22	24	20
University/college of higher education/Open University	16	18	22	9	8	18	27	18	12	17
Where I work	15	15	15	19	9	22	12	9	17	14
Adult education centre/evening institute/WEA	7	7	6	6	8	4	5	9	8	7
Employer's training centre	5	4	5	7	3	6	3	3	3	5
Private training centre/hotel/conference centre	4	4	4	4	2	5	2	3	3	4
School	4	4	4	5	3	3	4	5	4	4
Community centre/leisure centre	3	1	3	4	4	1	1	4	4	3
Local ICT learning centre, e.g. Learndirect, UK On-line	2	2	1	2	3	2	1	2	2	2
Voluntary organisation/informal group, e.g. U3A	2	3	*	1	2	1	*	2	1	2
Skill centre/job centre	*	*	1	*	1	*	*	*	*	*
Other educational institutions	2	1	2	2	2	2	2	1	2	2
At home: informal learning/from book	6	8	4	6	9	4	3	8	6	6
At home: using a computer, CD ROM, internet	6	10	5	5	3	5	5	7	5	6
At home: structured correspondence/open learning	3	4	3	2	2	3	3	3	4	3
Other locations	3	2	3	2	4	2	2	3	3	3

Table 4.7: Length of time learners have been studying/expect to study their main subject, by gender, 1999 and 2002 compared

		2002		1999
	All	Men	Women	All
Base: all current/recent learners = 100%	2073	1015	1059	2044
Less than 1 week	4	4	5	5
1 week – 1 month	5	6	4	5
Over 1-3 months	8	6	10	9
Total – up to 3 months	**18**	**17**	**19**	**19**
Over 3 – 6 months	10	9	11	10
7 – 12 months	12	11	14	13
Over 1 – 2 years	17	17	18	17
Over 2 years	41	44	38	39
Don't know/can't remember	2	2	1	3

Tables 4.8 and 4.9 record the average numbers of hours spent per week by current/recent learners on their main/only learning. The important point to note is that this question always produces a bi-modal distribution showing the clear difference between the third who are studying for the typical one class, one evening a week, people who may be studying for a full or half-day a week and those who are doing heavier part-time courses. Ten per cent more

Table 4.8: Number of hours a week spent learning, by gender

		2002	
	All	Men	Women
Base: all current/recent learners = 100%	2073	1015	1059
Up to 3 hours	29	24	34
4 – 6 hours	19	19	18
7 – 9 hours	9	9	9
10 – 12 hours	9	9	9
13 – 15 hours	4	5	4
16 – 20 hours	9	9	8
21 – 30 hours	10	11	9
31 – 40 hours	8	10	6
41+	3	4	2
Don't know/can't remember/NA	1	1	*

Figure 4.2 Number of hours spent on learning per week, by gender

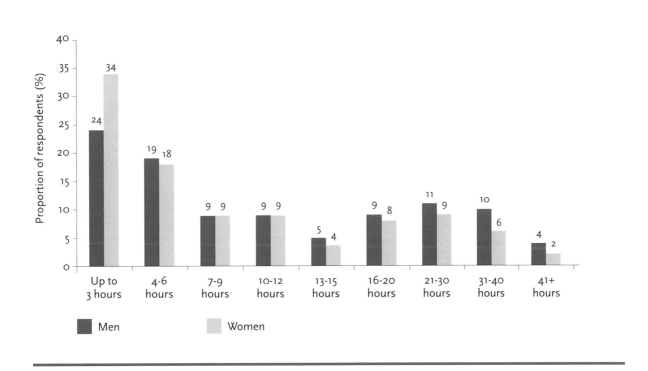

women are studying for up to three hours a week while more men are spending more time per week, sometimes effectively full-time, for the time period of the course.

Table 4.9 analyses the time-cost of learning against people's employment status. There is little difference between employment groups among those studying for time periods of less than three months: the proportions range from 18% to 20%. Nearly one-third (31%) of those who are unemployed and who are not working are studying for between three months and one year. Substantial proportions of those working part-time (35%), those working full-time (33%) and those not working (32%) are studying for over two years, as are 53% of those who are retired.

The differences appear more clearly in relation to the number of hours a week studied. One half of retired people study for 'up to three hours a week', with three quarters of them studying for up to six hours altogether. Time pressures are likely to be greatest for people working part-time, many of them women. One third of those working part-time study for up to three hours a week with over half (55%) studying for up to six hours, slightly more than the 49% of those working full-time. Those who are unemployed either study for up to six hours (30%) or for significantly longer hours: 16% for 16-20 hours and 31% for 21 hours or more.

Table 4.9: Length of time learners have been studying/expect to study their main/only subject, and hours a week they spend studying, by employment status

	All	Full-time	Part-time	Unemployed	Not working	Retired
Base: all current/recent learners = 100%	2073	1041	290	86	226	225
Less than 1 week	4	5	6	5	3	4
1 week – 1 month	5	7	3	4	3	3
Over 1-3 months	8	8	10	10	12	11
Over 3 – 6 months	10	9	11	13	15	8
7 – 12 months	12	13	14	18	16	7
Over 1 – 2 years	17	18	18	18	16	9
Over 2 years	41	33	35	30	32	53
Don't know/can't remember	2	2	2	3	2	4

Table 4.10: Number of hours a week spent learning, by employment status

	All	Full-time	Part-time	Unemployed	Not working	Retired
Base: all current/recent learners = 100%	2073	1041	290	86	226	225
Up to 3 hours	29	29	34	17	36	49
4 – 6 hours	19	20	21	13	19	23
7 – 9 hours	9	10	6	6	9	9
10 – 12 hours	9	10	10	4	10	6
13 – 15 hours	4	4	3	7	5	3
16 – 20 hours	9	7	9	16	9	4
21 – 30 hours	10	7	9	17	9	1
31 – 40 hours	8	8	6	14	4	1
41+	3	4	1	5	1	2
Don't know/can't remember/NA	1	1	1	–	–	2

The role of qualifications

Having identified their main or only subject of learning, respondents were asked whether or not they are or were aiming for a qualification. Since 1999, the proportion of learners aiming for a qualification has remained relatively stable, rising by only 2% from 64% to 66%. One in eight learners are studying for a degree, 10% are working towards an NVQ/SVQ, and 9% of adults are studying for 'other' qualifications (Table 4.10).

Among groups most likely to be aiming for a qualification are the young (96% of 17-19-year-olds, 91% of 20-24-year-olds, 75% of 24-34-year-olds); black (94%) and Asian (77%) adults; adults learning for education/progression (94%) and work related reasons (75%); those adults whose mother tongue is not English (79%); those whose highest qualification is at level 3 (79%) and the unemployed (77%). Groups least likely to be aiming for a qualification are older adults (26% of those aged 75 and over, 33% of 65-74-year-olds, 40% of 55-64-year-olds); the retired (29%); and those who highest qualification is at level 1 or below (42%).

For the first time in 2002, the survey has separately recorded the proportion of adults working towards newer vocational qualifications such as first aid, food and hygiene and health and safety certificates, often workplace based. Employers are often required to provide their staff with access to these opportunities as a means of ensuring certain standards within the workplace, and as such provide an arena where adults who might otherwise be reluctant to participate become involved in learning. It is to be hoped that this exposure to learning activity not only provides individuals with the motivation to continue learning, but also convinces employers of the value of learning beyond that which they are required to provide. Training facilities and agreements made with local training providers could then be utilised further to include a wider range of learning activities for those in work.

The list of options, which has evolved over time, was restructured in 2002 to ask about both the type and level of qualification. The list was also amended to replace those qualifications no longer available with more recently developed qualifications such as foundation degrees. In the attempt to make the list as comprehensive as possible, it is inevitable that a long list of qualifications has been produced, many of which are aimed for by only a small proportion of respondents. The additions made to the question have stretched it to its limits and it is hoped that the establishment of the English local Labour Force Survey should remove the need for such complexity within the survey in the future. Table 4.10 includes all qualifications mentioned by at least 1% of respondents. Those mentioned by less than 1% included Open College Network (OCN) credits, Foundation Degree, Modern Apprenticeship, ONC/OND, overseas qualifications, HGV licence and other post-graduate qualifications.

Table 4.11: Qualifications, if any, learners are/were aiming for, 1996, 1999 and 2002 compared

	2002	1999	1996
Base: all current/recent learners = 100%	2073	2044	1892
All aiming for qualifications	66	64	65
All not aiming for qualifications	34	36	35
Qualifications aimed for:			
GCSE grades A*-C/SCE Credit Level Standard Grades	1	2	2
GCSE grades D-G/SCE Foundation Level Standard Grades	1		
A level, A/S level, S level/AVCE/Scottish Highers	3	4	5
RSA	1	2	3
City & Guilds	4	3	5
BTEC/SCOTVEC/SCOTEV	2	NSR	NSR
National or general BTEC/ONC or OND	NSR	1	2
Higher BTEC, HND/HNC	NSR	2	2
Diploma in Higher Education (DipHE)	2	5	5
Degree (BA, BSc, BEd)	12	10	13
Higher degree (e.g. , MA, MSc, PhD)	3	3	2
Nursing/medical/clinical qualification	2	2	2
PGCE or other teaching qualification	1	1	1
NVQ/SVQ	10	15	12
GNVQ/GSVQ	2		
HNC/HND	3	2	1
Workplace based qualifications (e.g. health and safety, food and hygiene and first aid certificates)	1	NSR	NSR
Other professional qualification	4	NSR	NSR
Other qualification	9	NSR	NSR
Don't know	5	5	NSR

Qualifications over 1% only listed
NSR – not separately recorded; NA – not applicable

Two thirds of learners, both men and women, are aiming for a qualification (66%), although more men than women report studying for a degree (14% compared with 10%) and for level 4/5 qualifications more generally (30% compared with 28%). Over half of learners under 54 are aiming for a qualification, although the proportions drop steadily for respondents over 25 (see Figure 4.3).

Figure 4.3: Current/recent learners aiming for a qualification, by age

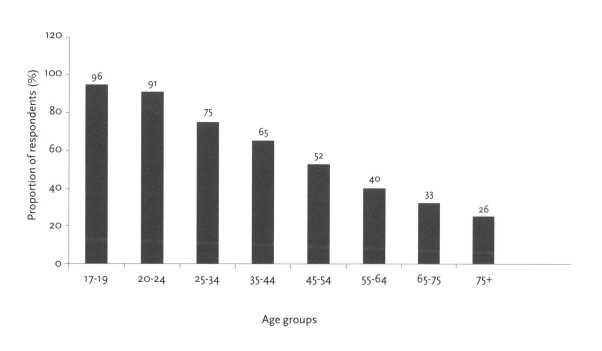

Seventeen-to-nineteen-year-olds are mainly aiming for A-levels (26%), a degree (19%) or NVQs (16%), while 44% of 20-24-year-olds are studying for a degree (Table 4.11). Older adults of working age are mainly aiming for NVQs, professional and other qualifications, while also continuing to aim towards more traditional qualifications such as City and Guilds. In terms of level, 40% of 17-19-year-olds are aiming for a level 3 qualification, while level 4/5 qualifications are most popular in all other age groups. The proportion of mature adults aiming for a degree declines after the age of 45. Teaching and nursing qualifications rank low, but are increasingly likely to be recorded as within a first-degree course.

As expected, both full-time and part-time learners are mainly working towards an NVQ, a degree or an 'other' qualification. Adults in these groups are also more likely to be working towards workplace-based qualifications than those who are not employed. Nearly a quarter of unemployed learners (23%) are working towards an NVQ, with 9% aiming for a City and Guilds qualification. Learners who are not working are mainly aiming for NVQs (14%), a degree (9%) or an 'other' qualification (8%).

One in seven unemployed learners are aiming for qualifications below level 2, while one in ten of those who are not working, the unemployed and part-time workers are aiming for qualifications at level 2. One in five full-time students are aiming for qualifications at level 3, as are one in eight of all part-time and unemployed learners. Over 70% of full-time students are aiming for qualifications at levels 4 and 5, as are a quarter of part-time workers and nearly a third of full-time workers (Table 4.12).

Table 4.12: Level and type of qualifications, if any, learners are/were aiming for, by age									
	All	17-19	20-24	25-34	35-44	45-54	55-64	65-74	75+
Base: all current/recent learners = 100%	2073	194	241	448	494	331	212	115	38
All aiming for qualifications	66	96	91	75	65	52	40	33	26
All not aiming for qualifications	34	4	9	25	35	48	60	67	74
Level of qualifications aimed for:									
All below level 2	4	6	3	5	4	4	5	2	–
All level 2	8	13	7	10	7	6	6	4	–
All level 3	9	40	7	8	6	5	3	2	5
All levels 4-5	29	32	68	36	25	17	15	6	9
Other	10	2	4	10	16	14	7	6	8
Type of qualifications aimed for:									
GCSE grades A*-C/SCE Credit Level Standard Grades	1	4	1	2	1	1	–	1	–
GCSE grades D-G/SCE Foundation Level Standard Grades	1	1	*	*	1	*	1	2	–
A level, A/S level, S level/AVCE/Scottish Highers	3	26	2	1	1	*	*	–	2
RSA	1	–	–	1	2	3	1	1	2
City & Guilds	4	3	2	4	5	5	5	3	–
BTEC/SCOTVEC/SCOTEV	2	4	3	1	2	1	1	1	–
Diploma in Higher Education (DipHE)	2	3	2	5	2	*	1	1	–
Degree (BA, BSc, BEd)	12	19	44	9	8	3	4	2	9
Higher degree (e.g., MA, MSc, PhD)	3	2	5	6	2	3	2	1	–
Nursing/medical/clinical qualification	2	2	3	3	2	1	1	–	–
PGCE or other teaching qualification	1	–	1	2	3	1	1	–	–
NVQ/SVQ	10	16	8	14	11	7	6	1	3
GNVQ/GSVQ	2	6	5	2		*	–	–	–
HNC/HND	3	4	9	2	2	1	*	1	–
Workplace based qualifications (e.g. health and safety, food and hygiene and first aid certificates)	1	–	1	*	2	2	2	1	–
Other professional qualification	4	*	2	5	5	4	4	1	–
Other qualification	9	2	3	8	11	11	7	4	5
Don't know	5	2	2	7	6	6	4	14	4

Qualifications over 1% only listed

Table 4.13: Level and type of qualifications, if any, learners are/were aiming for, by employment status							
	All	Full-time	Part-time	Unem-ployed	Not working	Retired	Full-time student
Base: all current/recent learners = 100%	2,073	1,041	290	86	226	225	201
All aiming for qualifications	66	67	68	77	63	29	100
All not aiming for qualifications	34	33	32	23	37	71	–
Level of qualifications aimed for:							
All below level 2	4	4	5	14	7	3	*
All level 2	8	8	9	10	11	3	6
All level 3	9	7	12	13	8	4	20
All levels 4-5	29	31	25	20	17	6	71
All Other	10	12	11	14	13	4	2
Type of qualifications aimed for:							
GCSE grades A*-C/SCE Credit Level Standard Grades	1	1	1	3	3	*	2
GCSE grades D-G/SCE Foundation Level Standard Grades	1	*	*	1	2	1	–
A level, A/S level, S level/AVCE/Scottish Highers	3	1	5	1	3	1	16
RSA	1	1	2	5	3	1	–
City & Guilds	4	5	3	9	4	2	1
BTEC/SCOTVEC/SCOTEV	2	2	2	1	1	*	3
Diploma in Higher Education (DipHE)	2	3	1	2	3	*	2
Degree (BA, BSc, BEd)	12	8	8	7	9	3	53
Higher degree (e.g. MA, MSc, PhD)	3	5	2	1	*	1	6
Nursing/medical/clinical qualification	2	3	4	1	1	–	2
PGCE or other teaching qualification	1	2	2	2	*	–	–
NVQ/SVQ	10	10	12	23	14	2	4
GNVQ/GSVQ	2	2	1	4	*	*	2
HNC/HND	3	3	3	4	1	*	6
Workplace based qualifications (e.g. health and safety, food and hygiene and first aid certificates)	1	2	1	–	1	*	–
Other professional qualification	4	6	2	2	2	1	1
Other qualification	9	10	11	3	8	4	2
Don't know	5	5	6	6	7	9	*

CHAPTER FIVE

Qualifications and the National Learning Targets

In 1998, the Qualifications and Curriculum Authority (QCA), in partnership with regulatory authorities in Wales and Northern Ireland, began developing a National Qualifications Framework (NQF) to assist employers, learners, and the public in gaining a better understanding of qualifications, to illustrate how qualifications relate to one another and guarantee the quality of qualifications on offer. Qualifications in the Framework are arranged in six levels from entry-level awards to professional qualifications at level 5 (see Table 5.1)

Table 5.1 National Qualifications Framework				
Level of qualification	General		Vocationally-related	Occupational
5	Higher-level qualifications			Level 5 NVQ
4				Level 4 NVQ
3 advanced level	A level	Free-standing mathematics units level 3	Vocational A level (Advanced GNVQ)	Level 3 NVQ
2 intermediate level	GCSE grade A*–C	Free-standing mathematics units level 2	Intermediate GNVQ	Level 2 NVQ
1 foundation level	GCSE grade D–G	Free-standing mathematics units level 1	Foundation GNVQ	Level 1 NVQ
Entry level	Certificate of (educational) achievement			

Although the Framework is still in the process of being developed, it was considered desirable, within this survey, to map the qualifications which respondents hold against it. In Scotland, mainstream qualifications were brought into a single unifying Scottish Credit and Qualifications Framework in 2001. The NQF is currently being reviewed in the context of this and other key frameworks – the Framework for Higher Education Qualifications, the National Qualifications Framework in the Republic of Ireland and other European and international frameworks – as well as in the context of new initiatives such as developments in work-based learning, unitisation and credit, European transparency projects and the impact of ICT on learning and assessment.

New National Learning Targets for England were agreed in March 1999. The targets require that by the end of 2002 50% of adults between the ages of 18 and 59/64 who are in employment or actively seeking it, should have a level 3 qualification (equivalent to 2 or more A levels, an NVQ level 3 or an Advanced GNVQ) and 28% should have a level 4 qualification (i.e. an NVQ level 4, a degree-level qualification or a higher level vocational qualification). Scotland, Wales and Northern Ireland also published national targets. An important additional target was also set for England, requiring a reduction in the proportion of non-learners of 7% by 2002. This target covers all adults aged 16-69, except for those in full-time continuing education. The report of the 2001 National Adult Learning Survey, published earlier this year by the Department for Education and Skills reported that the government has achieved its target of reducing the proportion of non-learners by 7%, that is from 26% to 24%, one year early.

Although the NIACE survey is not an official measure of these targets, it was considered desirable to try and classify qualifications held according to the National Qualifications Framework, despite the difficulty of obtaining this detailed information from such a survey. By doing this, these survey results offer a measure of progress towards government targets and enable an assessment of their impact upon different groups of adults.

Overall, 28% of adults in the UK do not have any qualifications at all, roughly the same proportion as in 1996 and 1999 (Table 5.2). Sixty-one per cent hold qualifications up to level 2, 37% up to level 3 and 24% up to levels 4 and 5. Groups least likely to have any qualifications at all are: older adults (42% of 65-74-year-olds and 39% of those aged 75 and over); the retired (45%);, adults in socio-economic classes DE (49%); and those who left school at the earliest opportunity (55%).

If 17-19-year-olds, many of whom are full-time students, and those beyond working age are both excluded from the survey totals, 69% of adults hold qualifications up to level 2, 42% up to level 3, and 28% up to level 4. Although the definitions used are slightly different, the NIACE survey indicates that the level 4 target has been achieved, but that the government appears to be short of its level 3 target (by 8%). However, looking at specific age groups, across the entire adult population, the level 3 target appears to have only been achieved among those aged 20-24, while the level 4 target appears to have only been achieved among 25-44-year-olds.

Table 5.2: Level of qualification held, cumulative totals by age										
	Total	20-64	17-19	20-24	25-34	35-44	45-54	55-64	65-74	75+
Base: all respondents = 100%	4896	3687	250	336	887	1002	757	705	583	375
No qualifications held	28	21	10	7	12	16	28	41	58	61
All holding any educational qualifications	72	79	90	93	88	84	72	59	42	39
All holding qualifications below level 2	3	3	2	1	2	3	4	3	1	2
All holding qualifications to at least level 2	61	69	81	88	80	74	59	48	30	25
All holding qualifications to at least level 3	37	42	32	62	48	41	38	30	21	15
All holding qualifications to at least level 4/5	24	28	5	24	34	30	26	24	16	12
Qualifications at unidentifiable level	5	5	4	1	4	5	7	5	5	4
Don't know	3	2	3	2	1	2	2	3	5	8

Looking at those respondents who are in employment or who are registered as unemployed, regardless of age, 74% of adults hold qualifications up to level 2, 45% up to level 3 and 31% up to level 4. Again, although the definitions used are slightly different, the NIACE survey shows that the government appears to have exceeded its level 4 target, but fallen 5% short of its target for level 3. However, looking at working status, it can be seen that the targets appear to have only been achieved among those who are in full-time employment.

One of the concerns about National Learning Targets which focus only on particular sections of the adult population, is that the patterns exhibited in tables 5.2 and 5.3 continue to be reinforced, such that those who fit inside the definition of the target are given further opportunities to gain qualifications, while those outside it – older adults, the retired and those not working – continue to be disadvantaged.

Table 5.3: Level of qualification held, cumulative totals by working status								
	Total	In employment or unemployed	Full-time	Part-time	Unemployed	Not working	Retired	Full-time student
Base: all respondents = 100%	4896	2761	2008	566	187	739	1188	201
No qualifications held	28	16	15	18	19	37	55	1
All holding any educational qualifications	72	84	85	82	81	63	45	99
All holding qualifications below level 2	3	3	3	3	5	3	2	–
All holding qualifications to at least level 2	61	74	75	71	68	51	33	96
All holding qualifications to at least level 3	37	45	49	39	28	22	21	68
All holding qualifications to at least level 4/5	24	31	34	25	15	14	17	18
Qualifications at unidentifiable level	5	5	4	6	5	8	5	1
Don't know	3	2	2	2	3	2	5	2

Looking to the future, the Learning and Skills Council (LSC) in England has been given responsibility for raising the proportion of adults, between the ages of 18 and 59/64 who are in employment or actively seeking it, with a level 3 qualification to 52% by 2004. The LSC has also been charged with raising the achievement of the entire adult population, measured by the proportion attaining a level 3 qualification, and the proportion lacking the basic skills of literacy and numeracy, as well as with raising adult participation in learning. Details of the new targets are to be published shortly.

CHAPTER SIX

Motivations and outcomes

Motivations for learning

The key difference between schooling and adult learning is that while children are expected to spend time learning, it is, for adults, a matter of personal choice which has to be fitted into often complex lives, competing with other demands on time such as work, family commitments and other interests. Understanding what motivates adults to spend their time learning instead of on other activities is therefore essential in seeking to encourage wider participation.

Respondents were asked to identify, from a given list of options which had been developed on a series of similar surveys, those which best describe their reasons for starting their main subject of learning. The more frequently cited reasons were 'I am interested in the subject/personal interest' (34%) and 'I enjoy learning/it gives me pleasure' (31%). Around a quarter of respondents mentioned 'to help in my current job', 'to develop myself as a person', and 'to get a recognised qualification'. Learning 'in order to improve my self-confidence' often a commonly reported benefit of learning within qualitative studies, was added to the list of options for the first time in 2002, and was referred to by 12 % of respondents.

Table 6.1 shows how the individual reasons for starting learning, listed within the question, can be combined into four main groups. Overall 62% of respondents cited personal development reasons, 53% work-related reasons, 27% education/progression reasons, while 6% said that participation in their main learning activity was not really their choice.

Men are more likely than women to be learning for work-related reasons (by 5%) and are also slightly more likely to be learning as a result of employer or professional requirements. In contrast, women are more motivated by personal development reasons (by 3%) and by education/progression reasons (by 2%).

Table 6.1: Reasons for choosing main/only subject of learning, by gender and age

	Total	Men	Women	17-19	20-24	25-34	35-44	45-54	55-64	65-74	75+
Base: all current/recent learners = 100%	2073	1015	1059	194	241	448	494	331	212	115	38
I am interested in the subject/personal interest	34	33	34	39	39	28	27	33	42	47	49
I enjoy learning/it gives me pleasure	31	29	33	32	30	27	26	28	43	47	61
To develop myself as a person	25	24	25	20	24	26	30	25	17	18	21
To improve my self-confidence	12	9	15	8	10	14	14	14	11	9	5
To meet people	8	7	8	9	14	7	5	6	9	11	11
All giving personal development reasons	**62**	**61**	**64**	**63**	**67**	**57**	**56**	**62**	**71**	**80**	**88**
To help in my current job	26	28	23	7	14	30	37	35	20	6	2
To get a job	17	17	17	44	40	21	9	7	3	2	–
To make my work more satisfying	13	14	12	7	12	17	14	14	9	4	5
To change the type of work I do	8	9	7	2	7	15	10	5	3	1	3
To get a rise in earnings	8	9	6	4	15	14	7	4	2	–	–
To get a promotion	7	8	6	3	8	12	8	7	1	–	–
To get a job with a different employer	5	5	5	2	7	8	6	6	1	1	–
All giving work-related reasons	**53**	**56**	**51**	**56**	**65**	**66**	**58**	**52**	**31**	**12**	**8**
To get a recognised qualification	24	24	24	40	39	31	23	15	9	2	2
To help me get onto a future course of learning	6	5	7	16	11	7	6	2	2	1	3
All giving education/progression reasons	**27**	**26**	**28**	**48**	**46**	**34**	**25**	**16**	**12**	**3**	**5**
Not really my choice – employer requirement	4	5	4	*	2	5	7	5	6	2	–
Not really my choice – professional requirement	2	2	1	1	*	3	3	2	–	2	–
Not really my choice – benefit requirement	*	*	*	–	–	–	*	*	1	–	5
Only type of learning available	*	*	*	–	–	–	*	*	–	1	–
All giving 'not my choice' as a reason	**6**	**7**	**6**	**1**	**2**	**7**	**10**	**7**	**7**	**5**	**5**
As a result of participating in another activity	3	2	3	2	1	2	2	3	6	4	4
Don't know	2	2	2	3	1	1	2	2	1	6	3

A respondent's age has a stronger impact upon their motivation to learn than their gender (Figure 6.1). In general, work-related reasons become increasingly important for individuals until they reach their thirties (66%), after which they become less so. This decline in importance is particularly steep for adults aged 55 and over, many of whom are approaching the end of their working lives and are becoming less motivated by work-related factors. Learning in order 'to get a job', is an exception to this pattern. It is most important for those 17-19-year-olds (44%), after which it declines in importance across all age groups.

In contrast, the importance of personal development reasons for learning generally increases with age, although there is a 10 point drop between 20-24-year-olds and 25-34-year-olds (67% to 57%). Within this grouping, personal interest in their subject and learning for pleasure are more important at either end of the age spectrum, while developing oneself as a person and improving self-confidence are more important for those respondents between their mid-twenties and mid-fifties.

Education/progression reasons for learning tend to decline in importance with age. Participation by those giving 'not my choice' as a reason for learning, is most evident among those in their middle years, with one in ten of all learners aged 35-44 participating as a result of an employer or professional requirement.

Figure 6.1: Reasons for learning, by age

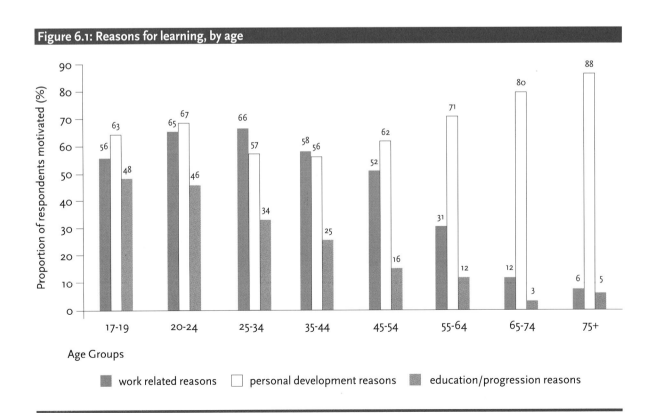

Reasons for learning in relation to socio-economic class and working status

The NIACE series of surveys has repeatedly shown that socio-economic class is a key discriminator in understanding adult participation in learning. Its impact upon people's motivation for learning, however, is less conspicuous.

There appears to be very little relationship between socio-economic class and the four groups of reasons for learning. Patterns do emerge, however, within some of the individual reasons. For example, around two thirds of both ABs and DEs cited personal development reasons for starting learning, yet hidden beneath this figure we can see that learning for pleasure and out of personal interest appears a stronger motivating factor for adults in the higher social classes, while learning in order to improve self-confidence is more motivating for those in the lower social classes. Similarly within work-related reasons, learning 'to get a job' becomes increasingly important for those in lower social classes (9% of ABs compared with 23% of DEs), while learning 'to help in my current job' (33% of ABs compared with 12% of DEs) and 'to make my work more satisfying' (15% of ABs compared with 7% of DEs) becomes increasingly important for those in higher social classes.

Work-related reasons are a major motivation both for those in employment (full-time 64%; part-time 55%) and for those seeking to be employed in the future (unemployed 66%; full-time students 60%). As expected, 'to help in my current job' and 'to make my work more satisfying' are key motivators for those in employment, while 'to get a job' is the main motivator for the unemployed (47%) and full-time students (51%).

Personal development reasons for learning are most important to the retired (84%), those who are not working (74%) and full-time students (71%). Learning for pleasure and out of personal interest is also important for these groups. Learning 'to develop myself as a person' and 'to improve my self-confidence' are most important for the unemployed and those who are not working.

Education/progression reasons are most important for full-time students. 46% are learning in order to get a recognised qualification and 12% are hoping to be helped onto future courses of learning.

Table 6.2: Reasons for choosing main/only subject of learning, by socio-economic class and working status

	2002 All	AB	C1	C2	DE	Full-time	Part-time	Unem-ployed	Not work-ing	Retired	FT student	1999 All
Base: all current/recent learners =100%	2073	541	759	397	376	1041	290	86	226	225	201	2044
I am interested in the subject/personal interest	34	38	34	31	32	28	27	33	46	50	44	23
I enjoy learning/it gives me pleasure	31	37	32	24	28	25	27	26	37	52	38	4
To develop myself as a person	25	25	24	24	26	24	26	30	30	19	24	8
To improve my self-confidence	12	11	11	13	15	10	16	17	22	9	8	NA
To meet people	8	7	7	9	9	5	7	15	9	13	13	1
All giving personal development reasons	**62**	**68**	**63**	**55**	**63**	**55**	**59**	**63**	**74**	**84**	**71**	**35**
To help in my current job	26	33	27	26	12	40	27	6	7	5	*	17
To get a job	17	9	17	20	23	10	16	47	22	1	51	10
To make my work more satisfying	13	15	13	13	7	17	11	14	5	4	11	4
To change the type of work I do	8	7	8	9	8	10	6	16	4	1	6	4
To get a rise in earnings	8	8	8	9	4	11	7	7	*	–	10	2
To get a promotion	7	7	8	9	3	12	5	2	2	–	*	5
To get a job with a different employer	5	4	5	5	6	7	6	9	2	*	1	1
All giving work-related reasons	**53**	**51**	**56**	**59**	**47**	**64**	**55**	**66**	**35**	**9**	**60**	**43**
To get a recognised qualification	24	23	27	22	22	26	23	30	18	2	46	9
To help me get onto a future course of learning	6	6	6	7	8	6	6	8	9	2	12	2
All giving education/progression reasons	**27**	**26**	**29**	**25**	**27**	**28**	**25**	**35**	**24**	**4**	**51**	**11**
Not really my choice – employer requirement	4	3	5	7	2	7	5	–	2	*	–	3
Not really my choice – professional requirement	2	4	1	1	2	3	3	1	*	*	1	1
Not really my choice – benefit requirement	*	–	*	*	1	*	–	2	1	1	–	NA
Only type of learning available	*	*	–	–	*	*	*	–	*	1	–	NA
All giving 'not my choice' as a reason	**6**	**6**	**6**	**8**	**5**	**9**	**7**	**3**	**3**	**3**	**1**	**4**

	2002 All	AB	C1	C2	DE	Full-time	Part-time	Unem-ployed	Not work-ing	Retired	FT student	1999 All
As a result of participating in another activity	3	4	2	2	2	2	2	1	5	5	1	NA
Don't know	2	2	1	2	3	1	3	1	2	4	1	NA

Interrelationships between reasons for starting learning

In both the 1996 and 1999 surveys, respondents were asked to identify one reason, from the given list, which best described why they had started their main/only subject of learning. In 2002 however, respondents were allowed to identify as many responses as they thought relevant. While this difference makes it difficult to compare results over the series, it does have the advantage of demonstrating the complexity of factors that encourage adults to learn (see Table 6.2). For example, in 1999 'I enjoy learning' and 'to make my work more satisfying' were both identified as the main reason for starting learning by 4% of respondents. However, in 2002, when respondents were able to identify a range of reasons, 13% referred to making their work more satisfying, while a much larger 31% referred to enjoying learning, reflecting its importance as an underlying factor in encouraging adults to learn.

Table 6.3 shows again how adult learners are rarely motivated by just a single factor, but will often only begin learning when a range of factors come together. For example two thirds of those who identified education/progression reasons for starting learning also cited personal development and work-related reasons. In the same way half of those who identified work-related reasons for starting learning also cited personal development while a third cited education/progression reasons.

Table 6.3: Interrelationships between reasons for starting main subject of learning					
	Total	Personal development reasons	Education/ progression reasons	Work related reasons	Not my choice
Base: all current/recent learners = 100%	2073	1295	564	1105	134
All giving personal development reasons	62	100	66	51	15
All giving education/progression reasons	27	29	100	34	8
All giving work-related reasons	53	43	67	100	28
All giving 'not my choice' as a reason	6	2	2	3	100

To illustrate this in more detail, Figure 6.2 takes all those respondents who identified personal development reasons for learning and provides a breakdown of all the other reasons identified by this group. The diagram shows that a quarter of respondents who identified personal development reasons also mentioned learning in order to get a recognised qualification, while 19% also mentioned wanting to be helped in their current job.

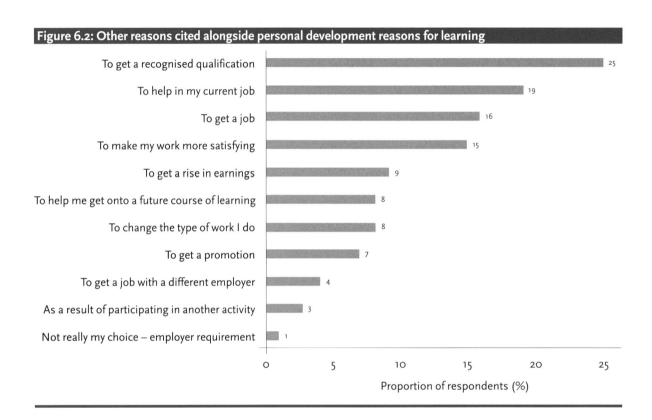

Figure 6.2: Other reasons cited alongside personal development reasons for learning

Attitudes to learning

Previous studies have shown that when asked, over 90% of adults say that they believe 'learning is something people do throughout their lives'. Yet this high level of appreciation of learning sits uncomfortably alongside a participation rate which shows that one in four of the population still believe that learning is not for them. In order to assist understanding of this situation an extensive series of attitude scales have been developed, concerning attitudes to schooling, to learning and training as adults and to work. Experience has shown that a number of the attitude statements represent some of the main attitudes which are of interest to policy makers and a number of key ones have been selected for continued use within this series of studies.

In 2002, respondents were asked to what extent they agreed or disagreed with each of the following statements:

> ... 'Learning is enjoyable for its own sake'[1]
> ... 'I am confident about learning new skills'
> ... 'People who get trained find their jobs are more interesting'
> ... 'People who get trained at work end up with better promotion or better pay'
> ... 'People should not be expected to learn new skills for their career in their own time'
> ... 'There is not enough help and advice available about the different sorts of learning people can do'
> ... 'I don't see why I should pay for learning that is to do with my job or career'

Encouragingly, 81% of adults believe that, apart from the instrumental benefits that it can bring, learning is enjoyable for its own sake. Three quarters of respondents agree that people who get training find their jobs are more interesting and say that they are confident about learning new things. However, as in 1999, while 92% of current learners expressed confidence in learning new skills, the proportion drops to just over half (55%) among those who have not done any learning since leaving full-time education.

Current (79%) and recent learners (77%) are most likely to agree that people who get training find their jobs are more interesting. Current learners are also most likely to agree that people who get trained at work receive better promotion and pay (67%). Among other respondents however, the more recent their learning experience the less likely they are to agree with this statement. This may point to respondents having participated in learning for the purpose of seeking a promotion or a pay rise, which has not materialised once their learning has been completed.

The continuing decline in the proportion of adults agreeing that there is not enough help and advice available about the different sorts of learning people do is encouraging. This figure fell from 47% in 1996 to 40% in 1999. In 2002 it fell again to 37% reflecting, it is to be hoped, the benefits of recent improvements in the provision of advice and guidance.

Since 1999 there has been a slight increase in people who don't see why they should pay for learning that is to do with their job or career (by 3%) and of people who believe they should not be expected to learn new skills for their careers in their own time (by 2%). Those adults who have not participated in any learning since leaving full-time education were most likely to hold these views.

---

[1] This statement replaces another general phrase, 'learning is something people do throughout their lives', which was used in the 1996 and 1999 surveys.

Table 6.4: Proportion agreeing strongly/agreeing with given statement, 1996, 1999 and 2002 compared

| | 1996 | | | | | 1999 | | | | | 2002 | | | | |
	Total	Current learners	Recent learners	Past learners	None since full-time	Total	Current learners	Recent learners	Past learners	None since full-time	Total	Current learners	Recent learners	Past learners	None since full-time
Base: all respondents in specified group = 100%	4673	1074	818	1086	1696	5054	1125	919	1148	1815	4896	1130	943	1039	1747
Learning is enjoyable for its own sake[2]	93	97	96	95	89	94	97	97	96	89	81	87	84	82	74
I am confident about learning new skills	74	94	89	74	56	72	92	89	71	54	74	92	89	74	55
People who get training find their jobs are more interesting	72	80	77	74	65	73	74	78	76	68	74	79	77	73	69
People who get trained at work end up with better promotion or better pay	70	71	67	71	69	63	63	63	67	64	66	67	63	65	67
There is not enough help and advice available about the different sorts of learning people do	47	53	48	43	47	40	45	39	35	40	37	40	37	34	38
I don't see why I should pay for learning that is to do with my job or career	44	39	39	40	50	44	43	46	41	45	47	45	46	45	50
People should not be expected to learn new skills for their career in their own time	31	23	28	30	38	30	26	27	25	34	32	27	29	30	38

Life circumstances

Research evidence suggests that certain life circumstances can act as a trigger in encouraging adults to participate in learning. In order to examine whether such a link exists, respondents were offered a list of personal and family circumstances and asked if any of them applied to their recent or current situation. The question, which was originally asked in 1996 and repeated in 1999, was amended in 2002, by replacing the phrase 'I had an illness' as used in 1996 and 1999, with 'I had a serious illness' and by making the following additions to the list: 'I have started a new job/been promoted'; 'I have recently lost a partner/spouse'; and 'I have a new/increasing disability'.

As expected, the incidence of personal circumstances since 1999 is relatively stable. However, an improved job market has resulted in more people gaining or hoping to gain a new job or promotion, and fewer being made redundant or taking early retirement. There has also been an encouraging interest in family learning, expressed as 'wanting to help my children learn' from 7% in 1996, to 10% in 1999 and 11% in 2002. Since 1999, there has been an apparent increase in the incidence of illness and disability from 10% to 13%, perhaps relating to the change of wording.

By cross-analysing the answers and without implying any causal relationship, table 6.5 shows that shows that seven of the listed circumstances are related to groups with higher proportions of current/recent learners than in the total population (42%). The groups with the highest proportions of learners are those who want/wanted promotion at work (67%); those who have started a new job/been promoted (66%); those who have moved home/to a new area (60%); those who have been involved in a broken marriage/relationship (54%); and those who want/wanted to help their children learn (53%). Circumstances linked to groups with a much lower level of participation in learning than in the adult population as a whole are those with a new/increasing disability (27%), those who have recently lost a partner/spouse (29%) and the retired (29%).

The largest increases in the proportion of current/recent learners within groups experiencing particular life circumstances are: among the retired/those taking early retirement (from 22% to 29%), although this follows a drop of 11% between 1996 and 1999; among those who have been involved in a broken relationship (from 49% to 54%), building on an increase of 4% between 1996 and 1999; and among those who want to help their children learn (from 48% to 53%).

---

[2] The phrase, 'learning is something people do throughout their lives', was used in the 1996 and 1999 surveys, but was replaced by another general statement, 'learning is enjoyable for its own sake' in the 2002 survey.

Table 6.5: Relationship of participation in learning to recent life experiences, 1996, 1999 and 2002 compared						
	All to whom statement applies			Percentage of group who are current/recent learners		
	1996	1999	2002	1996	1999	2002
Base: all respondents = 100%	4673	5054	4896	40	40	42
I wanted/want to help my children learn	7	10	11	48	48	53
I have started a new job/been promoted	NA	NA	10	NA	NA	66
I have moved home/moved to a new area	13	10	10	59	59	60
I have started a family	8	8	7	39	42	44
I have taken early retirement/retired	7	12	7	33	22	29
I have a new/increasing disability	NA	NA	7	NA	NA	27
I had an illness (serious illness)	11	10	6	32	39	35
I wanted/want promotion at work	7	6	6	71	72	67
I have been involved in a broken marriage/ broken up with my partner	7	5	5	45	49	54
I have lost my job/been made redundant	7	4	4	45	46	44
I have recently lost a partner/spouse	NA	NA	2	NA	NA	29
None	52	43	45	39	38	37

Benefits of learning

Lifelong learning has moved up the policy agenda and there is an assumption that this is a 'good thing'. Yet exactly what the precise benefits of learning are and which sorts of learners are most likely to experience them is still largely unknown. The majority of existing research around the benefits of learning has a narrow focus upon the economic returns to education. However in 1999 the Department for Education and Employment (now Education and Skills) established a Wider Benefits of Learning (WBL) Research Centre to investigate the non-economic benefits that learning brings to the individual learner and to society as a whole. In Volume 2, Professor Tom Schuller discusses some of the Research Centre's findings and its work programme.

In order to contribute to this discussion, a question asking about the returns to learning was included for the first time in the 2002 survey. All respondents who had learnt in the last three years were asked to identify, from a given list of options, any changes or benefits that had happened or they expected to happen to them as a result of their learning. The list of options is closely related to that used in the question on motivations for learning (see Table 6.1), but also includes other benefits commonly identified in qualitative studies such as 'my health has improved', 'my family have become more interested in learning' and 'I am more involved in local events and issues'. The option of saying that they had not experienced any benefits as a result of their learning was also offered. An 'other' category was not included in the 2002 list.

Table 6.6 shows that the most frequently cited benefits experienced or expected as a result of learning are improvements in self-confidence (29%), personal development (29%), meeting new people and making new friends (26%), and gaining a qualification (21%). Between 5-15% of respondents report a range of work-related benefits experienced or expected, from finding work more satisfying (15%) and being helped in their current job (14%) to getting a job with a different employer (5%).

It is interesting to see that despite a national policy focus on learning as a means of improving the nation's economic competitiveness, personal and social benefits are much more frequently reported than the majority of instrumental benefits. This may be because instrumental outcomes may take longer to realise than expressive ones.

Surprisingly, one in every six respondents reports not having experienced any benefit from their learning. However, as Schuller points out (Sargant and Aldridge, forthcoming), this could reflect a range of possibilities. Learners may indeed not have experienced any benefits at all; alternatively they may have experienced benefits other than those listed within the question. It is also possible that respondents may have enjoyed their learning simply as consumption or that they are unwilling to attribute any benefits directly to their learning. Finally, it is important to remember that more than half of those questioned have not yet completed their learning and therefore may not yet have enjoyed its benefits.

Changes or benefits as a result of learning in relation to gender and age

The general pattern of changes or benefits experienced or expected from learning is fairly gender free, although slightly more women than men cite personal and family benefits while men are more likely than women to refer to work-related benefits – a similar pattern to that of motivations for learning. The greatest gender differences can be seen in relation to meeting new people/making new friends, mentioned by 23% of men and 30% of women, and in relation to being helped in their current job, mentioned by 17% of men and 12% of women. Men (18%) are also more likely than women (14%) to say that they have not experienced any changes or benefits as a result of their learning.

Respondents' age has a greater impact than their gender upon the changes or benefits experienced or expected as a result of learning. The pattern of reporting work related benefits generally exhibits an inverted U-shape, that is they are increasingly mentioned until the respondent reaches a certain age, after which they decline again. The age group at which the reporting peaks depends upon the particular benefit being considered. For example, 'getting a job' is most frequently mentioned by 20-24-year-olds (33%), while getting a promotion (16%), changing the type of work done (11%), and getting a job with a different employer (11%) is most frequently mentioned by those aged 25-34. Interestingly, 45-54-year-olds are most likely to mention finding work more satisfying (22%), perhaps reflecting a difference in how work is valued in later life.

Education/progression benefits of learning are reported or expected most frequently by those aged 20-24, where 42% report getting a qualification and 10% report moving on to a further course of learning. Personal development reasons such as meeting new people (43%), developing as a person (37%), improving self-confidence (36%) and enjoying learning more (23%) are also most frequently mentioned by 20-24-year-olds, as well as becoming increasingly important for respondents aged 55 and over.

Involvement in local issues is most frequently reported or expected by older age groups, the health benefits of learning are mentioned most by those at either end of the age spectrum, while having an impact on their family's interest in learning is most evident among adults in their forties.

The complexity of interrelated factors that encourage adults to learn is demonstrated in table 6.3 and figure 6.2. It would be logical to assume that, in the same way, adult learners also experience and expect to experience a complex variety of different benefits to their learning, some of which will be connected to their original motivations for learning, and others which will not. Table 6.7 goes some way to illustrating this complexity. For example, of those respondents who were motivated by work-related reasons to start their main learning activity, 23% now find or expect to find their work more satisfying, 22% have been helped or expect to be helped in their current job and 18% have gained or expect to gain a job. But as well as these work-related benefits 33% feel or expect to feel more self-confident, 30% have developed or expect to develop as a person and 27% have gained or expect to gain a recognised qualification.

In the same way, of those learners motivated by personal development reasons, 36% say they have developed or expect to develop as a person, 35% have improved or expect to improve their self-confidence and 33% have met or expect to meet new people; while at the same time 23% have gained or expect to gain a recognised qualification, 14% find or expect to find their work more satisfying and 12% have gained or expect to gain a job. Evidence such as this runs contrary to the idea of a divide between vocational and non-vocational learning, or between learning which has an economic benefit and that which has a purely personal benefit. Instead it is evident that many learning experiences are embarked upon because of a wide range of motivating factors, and can result in an even wider range of benefits, both intended and unexpected.

Turning now to those adults for whom participation in their main learning activity was not as a result of their own choice, it is encouraging that these learners are most likely to have been helped or expect to be helped in their current job (29%) and one in five find that their work has become, or expect their work to become, more satisfying. However, while involuntary learning can produce some beneficial effects, the survey findings suggest that it may be less likely to result in some of the wider benefits of learning that are so valued by other learners. For example, only

Table 6.6: Changes or benefits experienced or expected as a result of learning, by gender and age										
	Total	Men	Women	17-19	20-24	25-34	35-44	45-54	55-64	65-74	75+
Base: all current/recent learners = 100%	2073	1015	1059	194	241	448	494	331	212	115	38
My self-confidence has improved	29	28	31	33	36	30	27	31	24	21	25
I have developed myself as a person	29	28	30	22	37	32	27	28	25	29	31
I have met new people/ made new friends	26	23	30	36	43	28	16	19	26	29	37
I have got/expect to get a recognised qualification	21	20	21	24	42	26	21	10	11	4	2
I enjoy learning more: more aware of the benefits of learning, know I can learn etc.	19	19	19	19	23	18	17	18	21	21	29
My work has become/I expect my work to become more satisfying	15	16	15	4	16	18	19	22	9	4	9
I have been helped/expect to be helped in my current job	14	17	12	5	7	17	21	17	12	3	–
I have got/expect to get a job	13	13	13	22	33	19	8	7	3	3	–
I have got/expect to get a promotion or a rise in earnings	9	10	8	3	14	16	10	7	3	–	–
I have changed/expect to change the type of work I do	7	9	6	4	9	11	9	6	4	1	–
I have moved/expect to move onto a further course of learning	6	7	6	8	10	8	7	4	4	–	6
I have got/expect to get a job with a different employer	5	6	4	3	5	11	6	3	1	–	–
I am more involved in local events and issues	5	5	5	5	9	3	2	5	7	12	12
My children/my family have become more interested in learning	4	4	5	1	3	3	6	5	4	3	4
My health has improved	4	4	4	6	4	3	3	5	2	5	7
None	16	18	14	15	9	14	17	19	17	26	20
Don't know	2	1	2	1	1	1	3	2	2	1	2

17% say they have developed or expect to develop as a person and 15% say they that their self-confidence has improved or that they expect it improve, compared with an overall proportion of 29%. Ten per cent have met new people, compared with an overall proportion of 26%, and 6% say that they enjoy or expect to enjoy learning more, compared with an overall proportion of 19%. None of these respondents report being or expecting to be more involved in local events and issues. Twenty-four per cent say that they have not experienced or do not expect to experience any benefits at all.

Two thirds of the learners questioned within the survey reported that they were aiming for a qualification, yet table 6.7 shows that only a third of these have already gained or expect to gain their qualification in the future. What is interesting is that in general, those who are aiming for qualifications are much more likely to experience other benefits of learning than those who are not. For example, 18% of those aiming for a qualification have gained or expect to gain a job; this compares with only 4% of those who are not and may be explained by the fact that a qualification can provide a potential employer with evidence of knowledge gained or skill acquired. Similarly, 32% of those aiming for a qualification mention actual or expected increases in self-confidence, compared with 24% of those who are not, in part perhaps explained by the fact that a qualification also provides the learner with evidence of their achievements, thus potentially boosting their self-esteem.

Table 6.7: Changes or benefits experienced or expected as a result of learning, by reasons for study and qualifications							
	Total	Work related reasons	Education/ pro- gression reasons	Personal develop- ment reasons	Not my choice	Aiming for a qualifi- cation	Not aiming for a qualifi- cation
Base: all current/recent learners = 100%	2073	1105	564	1295	134	1258	704
My self-confidence has improved	29	33	39	35	15	32	27
I have developed myself as a person	29	30	37	36	17	31	28
I have met new people/made new friends	26	25	36	33	10	29	24
I have got/expect to get a recognised qualification	21	27	43	23	12	33	2
I enjoy learning more: more aware of the benefits of learning, know I can learn etc.	19	19	23	25	6	19	20
My work has become/I expect my work to become more satisfying	15	23	19	14	20	15	16
I have been helped/expect to be helped in my current job	14	22	15	11	29	13	17
I have got/expect to get a job	13	18	23	12	9	18	4
I have got/expect to get a promotion or a rise in earnings	9	15	15	8	11	12	5
I have changed/expect to change the type of work I do	7	12	12	7	5	9	5
I have moved/expect to move onto a further course of learning	6	9	13	8	3	9	3
I have got/expect to get a job with a different employer	5	9	9	5	2	8	1
I am more involved in local events and issues	5	5	7	7	–	5	6
My children/my family have become more interested in learning	4	3	5	6	1	3	6
My health has improved	4	3	3	5	1	3	5
None	16	11	9	14	24	13	19
Don't know	2	2	1	2	1	2	1

CHAPTER SEVEN

Barriers to learning

The recent policy focus upon widening participation has resulted in considerable efforts being placed into understanding and dealing with the obstacles that prevent adults from participating in all forms of adult learning, as well as into supporting those who have successfully begun their learning. For example, within the field of adult and community learning, the Adult and Community Learning Fund has supported over 400 projects in developing and demonstrating ways of reaching new learners, engaging them in imaginative and innovative learning activities and supported progression. An impact study undertaken by the Institute for Employment Studies reported that all projects were successful at reaching new learners, with 20% of projects reaching 200 or more learners (Tyers and Aston, 2002). A range of other programmes and funding streams have also been introduced to widen participation in further education, higher education and work-based learning. This chapter focuses on what adult learners say about the barriers they face when commencing learning and the obstacles they encounter throughout their learning experience.

Retention

The series of surveys has repeatedly shown that adults who have been successful learners in the past are much more likely to continue learning in the future. Retaining adults in their learning activities is therefore arguably at least as important as attracting them to learn in the first instance.

At the time of interview, more women (38%) than men (33%) had already completed their main learning activity (36% overall), 59% were still studying and 5% had given up before the end of their study (Table 7.1). Those who had given up before the end of their learning activity generally appear in greater proportions in categories often associated with educational disadvantage. In percentage order, those dropping out include: 12% of adults aged 75 and over; 12% of socio-economic classes DE; 11% of unemployed adults; 9% of those whose highest level qualification is at level 2 or below; 9% of those who are not working; 9% of those with no telephone; and 9% of 17-19-year-olds.

These findings pose several challenges regarding the provision of appropriate information, advice and guidance to help learners find the right course, and the provision of appropriate support throughout the learning experience in order to improve retention. Adults within the groups listed above are already less likely to participate in learning than much of the rest of the adult population. If their learning experience is unsuccessful causing them to drop-out, their likelihood of participation in the future is reduced even further.

Table 7.1: Proportion of current/recent learners giving up before the end of the course, by gender			
	All	Men	Women
Base: all current/recent learners = 100%	2073	1015	1059
Completed the course	36	33	38
Gave up before the end	5	5	5
Still studying	59	61	57

Main factors preventing learning these days

Qualitative and quantitative research has identified a wide range of barriers to adult participation in learning. In her synthesis of American research, K.P. Cross (1981) categorised these barriers into three main groups:

- *situational barriers* arising from an adult's personal and family situation, such as time pressures and financial constraints;
- *institutional barriers* arising as a result of the unresponsiveness of educational institutions, such as inappropriate scheduling or content of provision; and
- *dispositional barriers* relating to the attitudes, perceptions and expectations of adults, such as believing that they are too old, too ill or too disabled.

In order to identify those factors most likely to act as a barrier to participation in adult learning in the UK today and how they impact differentially on certain groups of adult learners, respondents were asked to identify their likelihood of taking up learning in the next three years (see chapter 2 for analysis of this question). Apart from those who answered that they were 'very likely to learn' respondents were then asked the following question:

> From the following list, what, if anything, would you say are the main things preventing you from learning these days?

Respondents were presented with a list of options that included a range of situational, institutional and dispositional barriers from which they were asked to choose as many responses as they felt appropriate. The breadth of options listed was designed to offer a non-threatening method of responding so as not to prevent people from being clear about factors such as their age, infirmities or lack of interest in learning. The question was first used in 1996 but asked of a different group of respondents – all those not currently learning. The present respondent group was adopted in 1999, although the question remained the same. In 2002 several amendments were made to the list of options within the question. 'I feel I am too old' (13%) was separated out from 'I am too ill/disabled' (4%) and 'I know all I need to know' was reworded to read 'I feel no need to learn anymore', resulting in an increase in the proportion of respondents choosing this option from 3% to 9%.

The 2002 survey shows a similar picture to that found in 1999. Not being interested in learning remains the most frequently identified barrier to learning, although this has fallen from 27% to 25%. Among those showing least interest in learning are those with few or no qualifications (38%), those who have not done any learning since leaving full-time education (37%), those who are retired (35%), adults aged 55 and over (35%) and those who left school at the earliest opportunity (31%).

Work/other time pressures also present a considerable barrier, rising from 17% in 1999 to 20% in 2002. Among those most likely to be facing these pressures are respondents in full-time employment (36%) and those aged 25-44 (33%). Interestingly, 30% of adults who started their main learning activity for work-related reasons and 38% of those who are learning as part of an employer or professional requirement say that work/time pressures are major factors that would prevent them from learning in the future.

Barriers to learning tend not to be gender specific, with the exception of childcare arrangements/caring for others, where women (12%) are much more likely than men (3%) to be prevented from learning. The proportion of respondents mentioning childcare etc. rises to 18% for people with children aged 5-15, and 37% for people with children aged 0-4. Around one in five part-time workers and those who are not working also refer to childcare arrangements/caring for others as a factor preventing them from learning.

Those adults who have not participated in any learning since leaving full-time education include: 37% who are not interested/don't want to; 17% who feel too old; 15% who are prevented by work or other time pressures; and 11% who feel no need to learn anymore. The largest group of current learners who are not very likely to learn in the future say that nothing is preventing them from learning (38%), followed by 24% who are prevented by work/other time pressures. The pattern for recent learners is quite similar to that for current learners.

Table 7.2: Main factors preventing learning these days, by gender and learning status: 1999 and 2002 compared							
	2002						1999
	All except 'very likely to learn'	Men	Women	Current learners	Recent learners	Past learners	None since full-time education	All except 'very likely to learn'
Base: all except 'very likely to learn' = 100%	3820	1875	1945	511	676	945	1655	3956
Not interested/don't want to	25	27	24	8	11	25	37	27
Work/other time pressures	20	22	18	24	27	24	15	17
I feel I am too old	13	11	14	5	5	14	17	15
I feel no need to learn anymore**	9	9	9	5	7	9	11	3
Cost/money/can't afford it	7	7	7	9	10	7	5	7
Childcare arrangements/ caring for others	7	3	12	4	10	9	7	8
I haven't got round to doing it	6	6	7	4	6	6	7	4
I am too ill/too disabled	4	3	4	1	3	5	4	
I would not be able to get time off work	3	5	2	3	5	4	2	4
I don't feel confident enough	2	1	3	1	1	3	3	NA
Transport/too far to travel	1	1	2	1	2	2	1	1
I don't know what is available	1	1	1	1	1	1	1	1
I am worried about being out alone	1	*	1	*	–	1	1	1
I do not have the qualifications I need	1	1	1	*	1	1	1	1
I do not have the abilities I need	1	1	1	–	*	1	1	1
I am put off by tests and exams	1	1	2	1	2	1	1	NA
I am too nervous about the idea of starting learning	1	1	2	*	1	1	2	2
Not suitable courses are available	1	2	1	3	2	2	*	1
Lack of opportunity to learn in other tongue	1	1	1	*	1	1	1	NA
Other	1	2	1	2	2	1	1	3
Don't know	3	3	3	4	3	4	3	5
None*	15	16	14	38	19	9	9	17

Factors over 1% only listed. Responses chosen by less than 1% of respondents were 'I don't like being in groups of people I don't know'; 'I don't feel colleges/centres are welcoming'; 'I've tried learning in the past and it has been unsuccessful'; and 'lack of opportunity to learn in Welsh' (asked of respondents in Wales only).

* phrased as 'Nothing prevents me' in 1999

** phrased as 'I know all I need to know' in 1999

Table 7.3 summarises the main reasons preventing learning these days, recording only those which rate 2% or more, analysed by employment status. Some of these responses, such as "not interested/don't want to" and "None" of the factors prevent me, give few clues as to how to stimulate such people into learning. However, focussing on more specific reasons, among those working full-time, over a third (36%) refer to work/other time pressures, 8% refer to the cost of learning and 7% say that they would not be able to get time off work. Among part-time workers a quarter refer to work/other time pressures, one in five (18%) mention child-care arrangements/caring for others and 9% refer to cost/money/can't afford it.

Among the unemployed the cost of learning is a major barrier (15%), while care arrange-ments are referred to by one in five of those who are not working. Among retired respon-dents, dispositional barriers are much more prevalent than situational or institutional barriers – 35% say that they are not interested in learning, 30% say that they feel too old and 13% say that they feel no need to learn anymore.

Table 7.3: Main factors preventing learning these days, by employment status

	All except 'very likely to learn'	Full-time	Part-time	Unemployed	Not working	Retired
Base: all except 'very likely to learn' = 100%	3820	1487	419	137	581	1110
Not interested/don't want to	25	20	23	21	25	35
Work/other time pressures	20	36	26	7	10	5
I feel I am too old	13	5	7	4	6	30
I feel no need to learn anymore	9	7	7	8	8	13
Cost/money/can't afford it	7	8	9	15	7	3
Childcare arrangements/caring for others	7	5	18	7	20	1
I haven't got round to doing it	6	7	6	9	10	4
I am too ill/too disabled	4	*	1	4	9	7
I would not be able to get time off work	3	7	3	–	*	*
I don't feel confident enough	2	1	4	3	5	1
None	15	16	15	16	13	12

Factors over 2% only listed

Ease of access to learning

In order to explore some of the above issues in more depth, respondents were asked further questions about ease of access to, and the funding of, learning. The accessibility of learning is an important issue for adult learners, particularly those who are learning part-time and need to fit their learning activities around work, family and other commitments. Technological advances and developments in open and distance learning have made it easier to engage in learning from the home or workplace, although the issue of access is still critical for those who need to travel to where their learning takes place.

In 1996 current and recent learners were questioned about the distance travelled and the time taken to get to their place of learning in order to assess the impact of geographical accessibility on different groups of learners. These questions were not included in the 1999 survey, but in 2002 it was decided to replace them with a question regarding ease of access, which had also been included in a survey undertaken in 1999 looking at the motivations for, and the barriers to, participation in adult learning across Norway, Spain and Great Britain (MOBA) (Sargant, 2000). Of course, as Sargant commented within the MOBA study, such a question leaves the interpretation of the answer in the hands of the respondent and ease of access is a wider issue than just geographical accessibility, but might also include factors such as car ownership, availability of public transport, suitable childcare facilities and the timetabling of provision.

In 2002, all respondents who had identified themselves as current or recent learners were asked how easy it is to get to where their learning takes or took place. Respondents were provided with a four-point scale ranging from very easy to very difficult, as well as the option of saying that they do not have to travel as they are learning either at home or work. Seventy-nine per cent of respondents say that they find it easy to get to where their learning takes place. A further 13% say that because their learning takes place at home or at work, they don't have to travel. Only 7% of current/recent learners say that it is difficult to get to where their learning takes place.

Table 7.4 compares ease of access between men and women, between those living in rural and urban areas and between current and recent learners. Slightly more women (80%) than men (77%) find it easy to get to where their learning takes place, although more men (16%) than women (11%) learn from home or work.

Learners living in urban areas (80%) generally find it easier than those living in rural areas to get to where their learning takes place, (73%). This is due to a range of factors, for example one in six rural households do not have access to a car and individual car usage is even lower leaving many rural learners dependent upon public transport. Rural areas also have less access to both public and private services resulting in learners being likely to have to travel further to their nearest learning provider (Payne, 2001). Perhaps as a result of these factors, rural learners (17%) are more likely than their urban counterparts (12%) to be learning at home or work.

Slightly fewer current learners (77%) than recent learners (80%) find it easy to get to where their learning takes place, although more current learners (15%) than recent learners (11%) are/were learning from home or work. What the findings do not tell us is whether those who have not done any learning in the last three years believe that they would find it difficult to access learning – the MOBA survey undertaken in 1999 reported that access is much less of a problem for participants than non-participants (by 14%).

Table 7.4: Ease of access to location of learning, by gender, type of area and learning status							
	Total	Men	Women	Rural	Urban	Current learners	Recent learners
Base: all current/ recent learners = 100%	2073	1015	1059	368	1705	1130	943
Don't/didn't have to travel: learn(t) at home/work	13	16	11	17	12	15	11
Very easy	51	51	52	46	52	52	51
Fairly easy	27	26	29	27	28	26	30
Net: easy	**79**	**77**	**80**	**73**	**80**	**77**	**80**
Fairly difficult	5	5	5	6	5	4	6
Very difficult	3	2	3	4	2	3	2
Net: difficult	**7**	**7**	**8**	**10**	**7**	**7**	**8**
Don't know	1	1	*	*	1	*	1

There is very little difference in ease of access between households with or without children, despite the fact that arranging childcare can often make access to learning more difficult. Differences do exist however across groups of employment status (see Table 7.5). Full-time students (93%) are most likely to find access to learning easy, while unemployed learners have greatest difficulty in accessing their learning (16%). One in five retired learners and one in six learners who are working full-time are learning at home or in the workplace.

Barriers to learning   95

Table 7.5: Ease of access to location of learning, by employment status

	Total	Full-time	Part-time	Unemployed	Not working	Retired	Full-time students
Base: all current/ recent learners = 100%	2073	1041	290	86	226	225	201
Don't/didn't have to travel: learn(t) at home/work	13	16	11	9	10	20	–
Very easy	51	50	54	42	56	51	51
Fairly easy	27	26	27	31	26	22	41
Net: easy	79	76	81	73	81	74	93
Fairly difficult	5	4	5	13	6	2	6
Very difficult	3	3	2	3	2	3	2
Net: difficult	7	7	7	16	8	6	7
Don't know	1	1	1	2	1	1	–

Some interesting differences appear when analysing ease of access by nation and region of the UK (see Table 7.6). Twenty-two per cent of learners in Scotland are learning at home or at work compared with a UK-wide average of 13%. While only 3% of learners in Northern Ireland are learning at home or work, over 90% say that they find it easy to get to where their learning takes place. Within the English regions, learning at home or at work ranges from between 7% in the North East to 14% in the South West. However in the South East, a much larger proportion (24%) of all current/recent learners are learning at home or at work. Access to learning outside of the home or the workplace is easiest in the North East (87%) and most difficult in the Eastern and London regions (10%).

Table 7.6: Ease of access to location of learning, by nations and regions of the UK

	Base: all current/ recent learners = 100%	Don't/didn't have to travel: learn(t) at home/work	Easy to get to where learning takes/took place	Difficult to get to where learning takes/ took place
Total	2073	13	79	7
England	1711	13	79	8
Wales	94	12	82	6
Scotland	211	22	73	5
Northern Ireland	58	3	91	6
North East	127	7	87	6
North West	251	11	80	7
Yorkshire & Humberside	214	11	81	8
East Midlands	189	13	79	7
West Midlands	187	9	82	8
Eastern	145	12	77	10
London	223	9	81	10
South East	228	24	68	8
South West	147	14	77	7

NB Percentages are horizontal

Funding of learning

The provision of learning continues to be financed by a mix of sources: individual learners, employers and government or publicly funded bodies such as local authorities and the Learning and Skills Council. The balance of this funding varies for different sorts of learners involved in different types of provision, with more assistance provided for learners involved in formal provision.

Many learning providers also offer concessions and fee remission for some groups of adult learners. The 2000-01 Fees Survey (Aldridge, 2001) undertaken by NIACE into the fee levels charged to part-time adult students by LEAs and Colleges shows that many providers make 'special offers' to encourage new learners to participate and existing learners to enrol on more and different courses. Most providers also offer concessionary rates to particular categories of learners, with the most generous concessions offered to the unemployed, those on means-tested benefits and adults with learning difficulties.

Since the last major survey was undertaken in 1999, the Learning and Skills Council has taken responsibility for the funding and planning of post-16 education. Individual Learning Accounts have been introduced and subsequently suspended and all adults who want to improve their literacy and numeracy skills have been provided with an entitlement to free training.

The proportion of learners who do not have to pay fees has risen slightly from 26% in 1999 to 28% in 2002. A third of learners pay their own fees, with an additional 6% being helped by family members, double that of 1999. More women (36%) than men (30%) pay their own fees, although this gap has narrowed since 1999. Both employer-funded provision of learning and employer contributions to outside fees, of which men (25%) receive a greater share than women (18%), have fallen by 2% since 1999. The proportion of learners receiving local authority grants to help with their fees have halved from 8% to 4% while new options added this year – Individual Learning Accounts (ILAs) and 'help from my institution' were both referred to by just 1% of all learners.

Table 7.7: Sources used for payment of fees, by gender and socio-economic group: 1999 and 2002 compared

	All	Men	Women	2002 AB	C1	C2	DE	1999
Base: all current/recent learners = 100%	2073	1015	1059	541	759	397	376	2044
No fees to pay	28	28	28	27	24	31	35	26
Myself	33	30	36	38	34	30	26	30
Family/relative	6	6	5	4	8	4	4	3
My employer/potential employer paid outside fees	14	17	12	16	16	16	6	16
Employer-funded provision of learning	7	8	6	9	7	9	3	9
Government Training Scheme e.g. New Deal	3	3	4	*	2	4	10	3
ILA (Individual Learning Account)	1	1	1	1	1	5	2	NA
Help from my institution e.g. access funds, bursaries etc.	1	*	1	1	*	1	1	NA
Local authority grant	4	4	4	2	5	4	4	8
Other government funding	5	4	5	3	5	4	7	5
Charitable Trust or other non-governmental organisation	1	1	1	1	1	*	1	*
Other	1	1	1	1	1	1	1	2
Don't know	1	1	1	1	1	1	2	1

Those in social classes AB and C1 are more likely to pay their own fees, while those in social classes C2 and DE are more likely to receive fee remission and have no fees to pay. Taken together, employer funding of learning is relatively evenly spread across social classes AB (25%), C1 (23%) and C2 (25%), while only 9% of DEs receive such support. This is due in part to the fact that only 19% of DEs are in employment but also a result of employers tending to invest least in the training and development of their lowest-skilled and lowest-paid employees.

Not surprisingly, employer support for outside fees is strongest for those working full-time (24%), although the gap between full-time and part-time workers has been reduced by 5%. There has also been a 6% increase in the proportion of part-time workers who do not have to pay fees. An increasing number of unemployed learners are receiving assistance through government training schemes such as New Deal (from 15% to 21%). Over a half of retired adults continue to pay their own fees, although many providers offer fee concessions to older learners (Aldridge, 2001). The proportion of full-time students paying their own fees has virtually

Table 7.8: Sources used for payment of fees, by employment status

	All	Full-time	Part-time	Unem-ployed	Not working	Retired	Full time student
Base: all current/recent learners = 100%	2073	1041	290	86	226	225	201
No fees to pay	28	24	31	32	34	35	25
Myself	33	31	34	22	36	55	20
Family/relative	6	2	5	5	3	1	34
My employer/potential employer paid outside fees	14	24	13	2	2	3	1
Employer-funded provision of learning	7	12	4	2	2	–	–
Government Training Scheme e.g. New Deal	3	2	4	21	6	*	3
ILA (Individual Learning Account)	1	1	2	1	1	–	1
Help from my institution e.g. access funds, bursaries etc.	1	1	1	–	1	–	1
Local authority grant	4	3	4	7	4	1	13
Other government funding	5	3	4	6	9	2	10
Charitable Trust or other non-governmental organisation	1	*	–	–	2	2	1
Other	1	1	–	4	1	*	3
Don't know	1	1	3	1	2	2	1

doubled over the past three years from 11% to 20%, while the proportion receiving local authority grants has fallen considerably from 42% to 13%.

Adults at either end of the age spectrum are least likely to have to pay fees, either because at the younger end they still remain within initial education for which no fees apply, or because of fee remission at the older end. Support from family is highest among the conventional student age groups of 17-19 (21%) and 20-44 (25%). Employer support is highest among middle age groups but declines for those adults aged 45 and over. Although a drop in employer support would be expected for those beyond the retirement age, reduced employer support for adults aged 45-54 may reflect age discrimination in training and development among employers.

Figure 7.1: Three main sources of funding for learning, by age

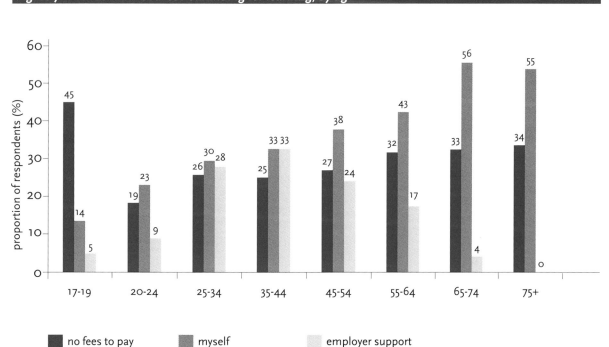

In the past the lack of consistency in the provision of discretionary grants for adult learners has been problematic. Following the introduction of the Learning and Skills Council and a new regional structure, it will be important to monitor whether the distribution of student financial support becomes more equitable. Table 7.9 shows variation is financial support across English Government Office regions. Employer support is highest in the North East (29%) and the South West (26%), and lowest in London (14%). The funding of learning activities as part of government training schemes such as New Deal is highest in the Eastern region (9%).

Table 7.9: Sources used for payment of fees, by English region

	All	North East	North West	Yorkshire & Humberside	East Midlands	West Midlands	Eastern	London	South East	South West
Base: all current/recent learners = 100%	2073	127	251	214	189	187	145	223	228	147
No fees to pay	28	24	30	30	29	26	27	30	30	24
Myself	33	28	34	29	36	30	31	38	37	34
Family/relative	6	5	2	5	6	11	5	9	6	5
My employer/potential employer paid outside fees	14	19	14	10	15	15	15	10	17	20
Employer-funded provision of learning	7	10	8	13	3	8	3	4	4	6
Government Training Scheme e.g. New Deal	3	6	3	1	4	4	9	3	1	2
ILA (Individual Learning Account)	1	1	1	1	1	–	1	1	2	4
Help from my institution e.g. access funds, bursaries etc.	1	1	1	1	–	2	1	–	1	–
Local authority grant	4	4	3	5	4	5	3	5	2	3
Other government funding	5	4	4	7	6	4	5	2	3	5
Charitable Trust or other non-governmental organisation	1	2	1	1	–	1	–	*	–	1
Other	1	1	1	1	2	1	2	1	–	1
Don't know	1	3	1	1	1	2	2	1	*	3

As well as fees, participation in learning can involve a range of additional costs. In particular, the continued growth of part-time learning, and greater use of new technologies often results in more of the costs of learning been born by the learner. Respondents were asked the following question:

> Sometimes learning can have other costs apart from fees. The following are some of the costs that people can experience when they do some learning. Thinking about your main learning of the subject, has it led or did it lead to any costs like these?

It is encouraging that half of all learners, both men and women, say that their learning has not resulted in any additional costs. This figure represents an increase of 7% since 1999. Childcare costs do not rank high overall but are mentioned by 2% of women compared with less than 0.5% of men, rising to 4% for those with children aged 0-4 and 3% for those with children aged 5-15.

The two most significant additional costs are travel costs and costs of equipment. Travel costs, reported by 31% of learners in both 1999 and 2002 are mentioned most frequently by full-time students (60%), those aged 17-24 (45%), and the unemployed (39%). High proportions of black (47%) and Asian (37%) adults also experience additional travel costs.

The proportion of respondents mentioning equipment costs fell by 9% from 37% in 1999 to 28% in 2002. This includes a 9% drop among full-time workers, a 12% drop among part-time workers and a 15% drop among those who are not working. It is to be hoped that this fall in equipment costs has more to do the increasing number of households who already have access to equipment such as computers and the internet, or an increased provision of IT equipment support by colleges or employers rather than reduced access for these groups.

Table 7.10: Other costs of learning, by employment status: 1996, 1999 and 2002 compared

	All	Full-time	Part-time	2002 Unem-ployed	Not working	Retired	Full-time student	1999	1996
Base: all current/recent learners = 100%	2044	1007	306	103	224	203	202	2044	1,892
No other costs	50	58	51	40	48	47	16	43	41
Costs of equipment	28	23	23	25	23	31	62	37	42
Travel costs	31	26	31	39	29	27	60	31	32
Loss of wages/ salary/overtime	2	3	2	*	*	–	4	5	7
Cost of childcare	1	1	2	1	2	–	2	2	2
Loss of benefits	1	*	1	–	*	–	2	1	1
Other costs	2	1	2	3	1	2	5	3	5
Don't know	5	4	5	7	6	8	4	6	2

CHAPTER EIGHT

The information divide: an update

Access to information and communication technologies (ICT)

It is generally assumed that the internet will play an increasingly important role in the development and delivery of lifelong learning. Similarly it has been assumed (SG) that ICT and the internet will improve access to the educationally disadvantaged, allowing such developments as the virtual college, learndirect (formerly the University for Industry) and the new NHS university. Issues of social inclusion now rank much higher on the nation's agenda and there is greater understanding of the significance of communications technologies in overcoming or reinforcing divisions in society. *The Learning Divide Revisited* (Sargant, 2000) provided evidence of unequal access to communications technologies among different demographic groups and regions. It argued that the potential information divide was as dangerous as the current learning divide, and that the two were likely to compound each other to the detriment of the proper provision of universally available lifelong learning as well as to the development of an active and inclusive democratic society.

Developments in telecommunications continue apace, and much of the recent focus has been on the potential of digital broadcasting. However, access to these new communications possibilities is still by no means widespread, though the government's various programmes for extending access to ICT through libraries, UK online, learndirect, and the New Opportunities Fund for community access to lifelong learning are starting to make substantial impact. The challenge is still very great: despite all the hype, the internet has not yet reached the majority of homes and is not yet easily available in all workplaces or learning centres.

There is also an increasing assumption that access to the internet can be taken for granted and an increasing number of information and service providers only work via the internet. Given the current level of penetration, at well under 50% of the adult population, this is quite dangerous to democracy as it increases social exclusion both explicitly and implicitly. The internet is, of course, an important new tool for lifelong learning, both for industry and for education and training, but there is not yet enough evidence about the best way to use and develop it, nor is much research going on about how its new facilities, particularly interactivity, can best be utilised.

This year's survey, with interviewing carried out in February 2002, records just 41% of individuals in total saying they have regular access to the internet. These figures are very similar to the

Office of National Statistics' survey of households which records 39% of households with access to the internet in the period October to December 2001. An earlier government survey, commissioned by the then DfEE in Autumn 2000, recorded 44% of individuals as having used the internet at some time and 37% as using the internet at that present time.

In the NIACE survey, respondents were asked which of a list of particular devices they had regular access to (see Tables 8.1 and 8.2). While the proportion with regular access to the internet has increased over threefold from 14% to 41% in the three years since the last NIACE survey, the demographic differences between regions, age and social class groups continue to be dramatic. More men than women continue to have access both to a computer/pc (7% more) and to the internet (9% more). However, while three quarters (76%) of the upper classes (ABs) have regular access to a computer, the proportion for the skilled working class (C2s) is only half (51%) and less than one third (28%) for the unskilled working class and those on benefit. (DEs). The significance of this is that computers and phone lines still act as the most important gateway to the internet and while regular access to a computer has increased from 35% in 1999, it is still only 53% in 2002. Neither do all people with computers have an internet connection.

New forms of access to the internet have not yet made an impact with all but 2% continuing to access the internet through a home computer/pc. There is little sign yet of the hoped-for market for integrated digital TV sets, which it was hoped, would also offer internet access, particularly to interactivity. The demise of ITV Digital has been a set-back to digital developments, and it is to be hoped that the new contracts being awarded to the BBC-led consortium together with the development of cheap digital set-top boxes will stimulate activity.[1] The Henley Centre's prediction that television would overtake computers as the most popular way to access the internet by as early as 2002 and that 'within a decade nearly 40 million Britons will be using their digital sets to access the world-wide web and send e-mails' (*The Mirror*, 8 February 2000) was clearly over-optimistic. As of now, access to free to air terrestrial digital broadcasting is very limited. This point will be returned to later in relation to the provision of educational broadcasting.

The proportion of survey respondents who have regular access to the internet reaches 50% or over for all the age groups up to 45, but then drops to 48% for 45-54s, 32% for 55-64s, 14% for 65-74s and 4% for 75+. While there is no difference between those in rural and urban areas (both 41%), the differences between nations range from 41% in England to 36% in Wales; and between the regions of England range from 48% in the North-East and South-East to 34% in the North-West and 37% in the West Midlands. The socio-economic class divide is serious, with two thirds (67%) of ABs having regular access, 55% of C1s, 36% of C2s and 17% of DEs. The other well-connected group, which is likely to cut across socio-economic class, is that of parents with children aged 5-15 (56%).

---

[1] The ONS figures for access were 13% compared with 14% for the 1999 NIACE survey. The 2001/02 ONS figures were 39% compared with 42% for the 2002 NIACE survey

Table 8.1: Proportion with regular access to listed communications technology, by gender and socio-economic class

	Total	Male	Female	AB	C1	C2	DE
Base: all respondents = 100%	4896	2381	2515	906	1398	1084	1509
Mobile phone	71	75	68	80	77	76	57
CD player	79	82	76	88	85	82	66
DVD player	26	30	22	33	31	28	16
PC/laptop	53	57	50	76	68	51	28
Internet/phone	39	42	36	64	51	34	16
Internet/BB	5	6	3	9	6	3	1
Any internet	41	45	38	67	55	36	17
None of these	12	9	15	5	7	9	23

Table 8.2: Proportion with regular access to listed communications technology, by age

	17-19	20-24	25-34	35-44	45-54	55-64	65-74	75+
Base: all respondents =100%	250	336	887	1002	757	705	583	375
Mobile phone	88	92	87	84	73	65	44	21
CD player	91	92	90	89	85	77	57	29
DVD player	45	44	37	35	26	15	6	2
PC/laptop	68	68	67	70	63	44	18	6
Internet/phone	47	50	48	51	46	31	13	4
Internet/BB	8	10	8	6	4	2	1	*
Any internet	50	55	53	54	48	32	14	4
None of these	2	2	3	3	4	13	30	62

The speed of penetration of some new devices is fascinating: the mobile phone is the contemporary example of this. In 1999, 30% of respondents had access to a mobile phone 'at home' with 18% having access at work, particularly men (25%). Three years later, three quarters of male and two thirds of female respondents have regular access to a mobile phone. Among the younger age groups, the proportion is around 90%. Mobile phones are offering real personal benefits in terms of flexibility and cost and when the third generation of phones starts to offer easy internet access at an affordable price, patterns of use are likely to develop and increase in unforeseen ways. The key indicator of this is the way that text messaging established itself, particularly among the young, using them in a way that the manufacturers did not even foresee. (If they had, they would have found a way to charge for it!) The next generation of mobile phones already offers visual access to calls and to the internet for £250, an invaluable service, for example, for the deaf. There will soon be learning packages for mobile phones. Their latest advertisements are already for photo-messaging.

Regular access to CD players is now high for all except the older age groups and the DE groups. While music of all sorts is the obvious driver for this, CDs are a valuable format for much adult learning and it is interesting that Tiscali, for example, includes 'How to learn Spanish' and 'Learning to Type' among their bonus offers. The next new device, building rapidly particularly among the young, are DVD players. A quarter of all respondents already have access to a DVD player, rising to one third among ABs. Access to DVDs among the youngest age groups is already over 40%. What is more disappointing to telecoms providers and to the government is the lack of take-up or interest in broadband, with its additional potential for interactivity. Only 5% overall access the internet via broadband. This rises to 9% among the AB socio-economic classes and to 10% among 20-24-year-olds. These two groups are likely to overlap somewhat.

What is the internet used for?

While access to technological devices is a necessary prerequisite to use, the key question for the future is how will people choose to use these new technologies. The issue for those interested in adult and lifelong learning is to know in more detail what the internet is being used for and whether or not it is or could be being used more actively for access to adult learning resources.

The ONS survey first asks whether or not individuals have 'accessed the internet at some time', and records 56%, an increase of 5% from January 2001, who say they have, with a narrowing of the gap between men (58%) and women (54%) (ONS, 2002). They then ask what respondents people have used the internet for and what they use it for most. Respondents are offered a set of categories of activities to choose from. The 2002 NIACE survey builds on the ONS survey categories by asking respondents who say they have regular internet access:

> Which of these listed activities have you ever use the internet for?
> Which of these activities do you mostly use it for?

The list of categories has been kept the same as the ONS, with the exception of the addition of two categories specifically relating to adult learning; 'finding information for my own education and training'; and 'learning on/off line'. The ONS question focused more on schools and did not separate adult learning, using the phrase: 'finding information related to schoolwork or education course'.

Table 8.3 compares activities the internet is 'ever' used for by respondents with those they 'mostly' use the internet for, analysed by gender. The final column in Table 8.3 shows the ONS proportions for 'purpose of use' from their October 2001 survey*.The NIACE pattern of answers indicating which purposes has the internet ever been used for is very similar to the pattern of ONS responses for the purpose of recent use.

Table 8.3: Activities internet ever and mostly used for, by gender

	Ever used for			Mostly used for			ONS 2001
	Total	Male	Female	Total	Male	Female	
Base-all with regular internet access = 100%	2006	1063	943	2006	1063	943	
Activities							**Purpose**
Communication:							
Using e-mail	76	79	73	37	36	39	73
Using chat rooms or sites	16	19	13	1	2	1	14
Information search and on-line services:							
Finding info about goods/services	58	62	54	7	6	8	74
Buying, ordering tickets/goods services	43	47	39	2	2	2	42
Personal banking, financial, investment activities	31	36	25	3	3	3	28
Using or accessing government/ official services	24	28	19	1	1	1	19
Looking for jobs or work	26	31	21	1	2	1	21
Finding information related to children's schoolwork	23	22	23	3	2	4	36*
Finding information for my learning/training	38	41	35	6	6	6	NA
Learning on/off line	22	26	17	2	1	2	NA
Down-loading software inc. games	30	39	19	2	2	1	22
Playing/downloading music	27	34	19	1	2	1	18
General browsing/surfing	69	74	63	21	24	18	56
Other things	8	10	6	2	3	1	3
None/don't know	8	5	11	9	6	12	NSR

*ONS: 'finding education related to schoolwork or education course'

When respondents were asked more precisely what they ''mostly' use the internet for, the percentages for most uses are extremely low with the exception of e-mail (37%) and general browsing/surfing (21%). The market for services is not yet well developed and government is clearly over-optimistic over the progress of its move to e-democracy. The assumption made on TV, radio and the press that most people can/will use the web to follow up their stories, get more detail or respond to them by e-mail is not only wrong but is excluding of many people. Similarly the BBC in moving much of its educational effort off-screen and onto the web, is denying potential access to educational stimuli and follow-up for the majority of its licence-payers.

There are some interesting differences by age group. While e-mail is used uniformly by a third or more of all age-groups, only 17-19 year-olds are into using chat-rooms or sites and down-loading music. Those aged 25 and upwards start to use it most for finding information about goods and services, with 4% of 35-44 year-olds both using it for buying goods and for banking or other financial services.

Table 8.4 Activities internet mostly used for, by age

	Total	17-19	20-24	25-34	35-44	45-54	55-64	65-74	75+
Base-all with regular internet access = 100%	2006	126	187	468	541	367	223	81	14*
Activities									
Communication:									
Using e-mail	37	38	43	38	33	37	40	38	46
Using chat-rooms or sites	1	8	2	1	1	*	1	1	–
Information search and on-line services:									
Finding info about goods/services	7	1	2	8	8	8	7	5	9
Buying/ordering tickets/goods/services	2	1	2	2	4	2	1	1	–
Personal banking, financial investment activities	3	–	2	4	4	2	3	2	–
Using or accessing government/ official services	1	1	–	1	1	1	3	–	–
Looking for jobs or work	1	1	2	2	1	1	1	–	–
Finding information relating to children's school-work	3	1	*	3	5	3	–	3	–
Finding information for my learning/ training	6	14	9	6	5	6	5	3	13
Learning on/off line	2	3	6	1	1	1	2	1	–
Down-loading soft-ware including games	2	1	4	2	1	2	–	1	–
Playing/down-loading music	1	6	3	1	1	1	–	–	–
General browsing/surfing	21	22	19	22	23	21	16	22	21
Other things	2	1	3	2	2	2	3	2	–
None/don't know	9	2	2	6	9	13	17	20	12

* please note small sample size.

On the positive side, 6% of individuals with internet access are 'mostly' using the internet for information for their own learning and this rises to 12% among current learners, with 3% of current/recent learners learning on/off line. Fourteen per cent of 17-19 year-olds and 9% of 20-24 year-olds are using the internet for information for their own learning and 6% of 20-24 year-olds are learning on/off line. This offers a minimum benchmark to build on, but the challenge is formidable and the risk of increasing the information divide is great.

A useful statistic comes from the Government's ONS survey, which continues to benchmark where people access the internet. They record 79% of individuals as accessing it from their own home. Second most important as the point of access is the respondent's workplace (35%) followed by another person's home (28%) and a school, college or other educational institution (22%). Other locations include an internet café/shop (9%), public library (8%), community/voluntary organisation or a government office (both at 1%).

While there is a welcome increase in access from home, it is clear that if more people are to be reached, other forms of access are necessary and important and that both public government and private initiatives are already playing a role in these developments.

The importance of broadcasting as a link to learning

The 'learning divide' is now well documented and there is increasing concern about its links with the 'information divide', clearly encouraged by lack of access to computers and therefore to the internet. To call this a 'digital divide' is only partly true: it is the same groups of people who tend not to have access to a pc, tend not to use libraries and cultural facilities, tend to come from lower socio-economic groups, and to have completed their education at too early an age as earlier chapters have made clear. The importance of maintaining high-quality access to universally available services such as libraries and the BBC and for this to be free at the point of use cannot be overestimated. If not, educational, cultural and social capital will continue to be unevenly distributed, as financial capital, of course, already is.

The 'digital divide' is a phrase being used indiscriminately about access to software offered in a digital format (e.g. the BBC's digital curriculum for schools), about the switchover from analogue to digital transmission of television and radio programmes, and
about specific digital channels, (such as BBC News 24, BBC3 and BBC 4) which are only available to those with digital equipment. There is still much confusion about the significance and benefits of digital broadcasting and the early, much-publicised demise of ITV digital has not helped public confidence. The vast majority of new sets being bought are still analogue and the market is not helped by the high cost of integrated digital television sets. The Communications Bill raises important issues in relation to the maintenance and regulation of public service broadcasting across all channels and providers, and the 2002 survey includes questions about access to a variety of television reception services, whether paying or free to air.

Table 8.5 shows the proportions of individuals who have access to different TV reception services. More than half the population is still reliant on analogue TV and on the BBC and Channel 4 for the bulk of its public service broadcasting and therefore for its educational components (note that Sky satellite television is now entirely digital, but that some analogue satellite television is still received here from other countries).

Table 8.5: Access to ICT/internet and to broadcasting by gender, socio-economic class and learning status

Base=100%	Total	Gender		Socio-economic class				Learning status			
		Male	Female	AB	C1	C2	DE	Current	Recent	Past	None
ICT											
Computer/pc/laptop	53	57	50	76	68	51	28	79	70	49	31
Internet via phone	39	42	36	64	51	34	16	60	53	36	20
Int. via broadband	5	6	3	9	6	3	1	9	6	4	2
Any internet	41	45	38	67	55	36	17	64	56	38	21
TV											
Digital satellite	21	23	19	21	22	26	16	22	24	29	19
Satellite nondigital	8	8	7	8	8	8	7	6	7	7	9
Cable nondigital	10	10	11	10	12	12	9	11	11	10	10
Digital cable	7	7	7	7	8	6	7	9	7	6	6
Digital set top box	3	3	2	3	3	4	2	3	3	3	2
TV built-in digital	*	*	*	*	*	*	*	*	*	*	*
No multi-channel	52	49	54	53	48	44	60	49	48	53	55

Among the multi-channel providers, Sky digital satellite television, with no educational obligations, has a commanding lead and withdrew its analogue service in 2001 without any major public reaction. It is important to note that access to multi-channel TV, both satellite and cable, is much more evenly spread across socio-demographic groups, with the exception of age. Older people, in particular, are still much more reliant on analogue TV, with 57% of 55-64s, 71% of 65-74's and 83% of 75+ without multi-channel access of any sort. However, the future pattern of the BBC-led replacement for ITV Digital is not yet clear and cheap digital set-top boxes are only just coming on the market. The decision to allocate the ITV multiplexes to a BBC-led consortium also puts pressure on the other public-service educational provider, Channel 4.

Despite earlier promises, the BBC in offering its new digital channels has as yet made no commitment to any additional educational programming for adults and indeed has withdrawn the Knowledge Channel, formerly named the Learning Channel, replacing it with BBC 4. BBC3 is being aimed at the younger adult audience, and both channels 3 and 4 are part-channels with their day times allocated to children's programming. It is not clear why the BBC has allocated both digital daytime segments to children. There are an increasing number of older people available during the day and stimulating daytime programming aimed at mature people could just attract more older viewers to sign up to digital.

If the government really wishes an early analogue switch-off then it is its older viewers who need to be wooed. There are many areas of educational, factual and cultural programming which are of particular interest to older people and could happily sit in daytime schedules as well as more targeted information, current affairs and consumer programming for older people. There are many more older people at home to view in the daytime than there are children, except in school holidays. This is apart from the need for major educational campaigns such as health, parenting, citizenship, media literacy, reaching the unemployed, and environmental issues, for example. It is the BBC that carries the major responsibility for public service broadcasting, and it is clear that until most people have access to digital delivery, their responsibility must be to continue to carry such a breadth of broadcasting on analogue screens and to ensure that it is then transferred to digital.

The role that on-screen broadcasting plays in offering ideas, stimulating access, in direct teaching, in linking in with other providers, and above all, reaching people at home universally and freely at the point of use is unique and offers unparalleled support to adult learners and lifelong learning. It is particularly important for the increasing number of older people who are much less likely to have multi-channel TV and adults probably need it more than the young who are now able to take the riches of the internet for granted through their schooling. The Communications Bill proposes the need for education for media literacy. This is first and foremost a task for the media itself and on mass channels.

RSGB's Omnibus survey and random location sampling method

Method

The information presented in this report was obtained as part of RSGB's General Omnibus Survey for March 2002. Appendix 6 contains a copy of the questionnaire.

Sample

The survey was based on a representative sample of c.5000 adults. They were selected from a minimum of 390 sampling points by random location method, which is described below.

Fieldwork

Respondents are interviewed at home by interviewers organised by SFR's Regional Managers according to RSGB's detailed instructions about the survey and administration procedures. The back-checking procedures that were carried out met the requirements of the Market Research Society Interviewer Quality Control Scheme (IQCS). The interviews took place during the period 13 February – 3 March 2002.

Data Processing

After coding and editing the data, weights were used to allow for sampling variation. The weighting scheme took account of the boost interviews in Wales by down-weighting the boosted region back to its normal proportion in the UK population. Details of the weighted and unweighted samples are shown in Appendix 4.

RSGB Random Location Sampling Method

A unique sampling system has been developed by Taylor Nelson Sofres for its own use. Utilising 1991 UK Census small area statistics and the Post Office Address File (PAF), the eligible area of the country has been divided into 600 areas of equal proportion. The areas within each Standard Region were stratified into population density bands, and within band in descending order by percentage of population in socio-economic Grades I and II.

To maximise the statistical accuracy of Omnibus sampling, sequential waves of fieldwork are allocated systematically across the sampling frame so as to ensure the maximum geographical dispersion.

The 600 primary sampling units are allocated to 25 sub-samples of 24 points each, with each sub-sample in itself being a representative drawing from the frame. For each wave of Omnibus fieldwork a set of sub-samples is selected so as to provide the number of sample points required (typically c.130 for 2,000 interviews). Across sequential waves of fieldwork all sub-samples are systematically worked, thereby reducing the clustering effects on questionnaires asked for two or more consecutive weeks.

Each primary sampling unit is divided into two geographically distinct segments, each containing, as far as possible, equal populations. The segments comprise aggregations of complete post-code sectors. Within each half (known as the A and B halves) postcode sectors have been sorted by the percentage of the population in socio-economic groups I and II. One postcode sector from each primary sampling unit is selected from each Omnibus, alternating on successive selections between the A and B halves of the primary sampling unit, again to reduce clustering effects. For each wave of interviewing each interviewer is supplied with two blocks of 100 addresses, drawn from different parts of the sector. Addresses are contacted systematically with three doors being left after each successful interview.

Interviewing is restricted to after 2pm on weekdays or all day at the weekend. To ensure a balanced sample of adults within effective contacted addresses, a quota is set by sex (male, female, housewife, female non-housewife)); within female housewife, presence of children and working status and within men, working status.

A guide to socio-economic class

Grade 'A' Households: the upper middle class

The head of a Grade 1 household is a successful business or professional person, senior civil servant, or has considerable private means. A young person in some of these occupations who is not yet fully established may still be found in Grade 'B', though s/he eventually should reach Grade 'A'.

In country or suburban areas, 'A' grade households usually live in large detached houses or in expensive flats. In towns, they may live in expensive flats or town houses in the better parts of town.

Grade 'B' Households: the middle class

In general, the heads of 'B' grade households will be quite senior people but not at the very top of their profession or business. They are quite well-off, but their style of life is generally respectable rather than rich or luxurious. Non-earners will be living on private pensions or on fairly modest private means.

Grade 'C1' Households: the lower middle class

In general Grade 'C1' is made up of families of small tradespeople and non-manual workers who carry out less important administrative, supervisory and clerical jobs, i.e. what are sometimes called 'white collar' workers.

Grade 'C2' Households: the skilled working class

Grade 'C2' consists in the main of skilled manual workers and their families. When in doubt as to whether the head of the household is skilled or unskilled, check whether s/he has served an apprenticeship; this may be a guide, though not all skilled workers have served an apprenticeship.

Grade 'D' Households: the semi-skilled and unskilled working class

Grade 'D' consists mainly of manual workers, generally semi-skilled or unskilled. It also includes non-earners: retired people who before retirement would have been in 'D' Grade and have pensions other than State Pensions, or have other private means.

Grade 'E' Households: those at lowest level of subsistence

Grade 'E' consists of old age pensioners, widows and their families, casual workers and those who, through sickness or unemployment, are dependent upon social security systems.

Notes on the tables

The sample covers the adult population of the United Kingdom, aged 17 and over. The sample used is specified in each table, and details of the weighted and unweighted samples are given in Appendix 4.

Figures in the tables are from the 1999 and 2002 RSGB/NIACE surveys unless otherwise indicated.

The 1980 survey was carried out by Taylor Nelson Associates; the 1990 survey by BMRB; and the 1996 survey by the GALLUP organisation.

Tables are percentaged vertically unless otherwise specified.

All tables are based on weighted totals. Researchers who wish to pursue any particular topic can obtain the necessary basic figures from the set of full analyses at NIACE.

In tables, * indicates less than 0.5 per cent but greater than zero, and – indicates zero. NSR indicates not separately recorded and NA indicates not asked.

Percentages equal to or greater than 0.5 have been rounded up in all tables (e.g. 0.5 per cent = 1 per cent, 36.5 per cent = 37 per cent).

Owing to the effect of rounding weighted data, the weighted bases in the tables may not always add up to the expected base.

In a number of questions, respondents were invited to give more than one answer: and so percentages may well add up to more than 100%.

Percentages are rounded to the nearest whole number. This may cause some mutually exclusive categories to sum to slightly more or slightly less than 100%.

Some sub-questions are filtered, that is, they are only asked of a proportion of respondents. Where questions are filtered, the base of relevant groups is indicated at the beginning of that table and percentages are derived from that base.

Regional analyses: inevitably, the number of sampling points in any one region is small. This fact should be taken into account when interpreting regional differences.

Analysis of weighted and unweighted samples

Sex, age, socio-economic grade

Base: All adults aged 17 or over	Unweighted		Weighted	
Total	5885	100%	4896	100%
Sex				
Male	2684	46	2381	49
Female	3201	54	2515	51
Age				
16-24	751	13	586	12
25-34	1015	17	887	18
35-44	1154	20	1,002	20
45-54	904	15	757	15
55+	2061	35	1663	34
Socio-economic grade				
AB	971	16	906	19
C1	1538	26	1398	29
C2	1275	22	1084	22
DE	2101	36	1509	31
Standard Region				
London	607	10	483	10
South East	914	16	695	14
South West	440	7	324	7
East Anglia	198	3	208	4
East Midlands	373	6	412	8
West Midlands	433	7	470	10
North West	541	9	586	12

Yorkshire and Humberside	469	8	515	11
North	309	5	344	7
Wales	995	17	241	5
Scotland	439	7	483	10
Northern Ireland	167	3	144	3

Regions

Standard Regions
1. Yorkshire/Humberside
2. North – Cumbria, Northumberland, Durham, Cleveland, Tyne and Wear
3. South West – Cornwall, Devon, Somerset, Dorset, Wiltshire, Gloucestershire
4. East Midlands – Northamptonshire, Leicestershire, Lincolnshire, Nottinghamshire, Derbyshire
5. South East – Essex, Hertfordshire, Bedfordshire, Buckinghamshire, Oxfordshire, Berkshire, Hampshire, Surrey, Sussex, Kent
6. East Anglia – Norfolk, Suffolk, Cambridgeshire
7. West Midlands – Hereford, Worcester, Shropshire, Staffordshire, Warwickshire
8. North West – Cheshire, Greater Manchester, Lancashire, Merseyside
9. Wales
10. Scotland
11. Greater London

Government Office Regions
1. Yorkshire/ Humberside
2. North East – Northumberland, Durham, Cleveland, Tyne and Wear
3. South West – Cornwall, Devon, Somerset, Dorset, Wiltshire, Gloucestershire
4. East Midlands – Northamptonshire, Leicestershire, Lincolnshire, Nottinghamshire, Derbyshire
5. South East – Buckinghamshire, Oxfordshire, Berkshire, Hampshire, Surrey, Sussex, Kent
6. Eastern – Norfolk, Suffolk, Cambridgeshire, Essex, Hertfordshire, Bedfordshire
7. West Midlands – Hereford, Worcester, Shropshire, Staffordshire, Warwickshire
8. North West – Cheshire, Greater Manchester, Lancashire, Merseyside, Cumbria
9. Wales
10. Scotland
11. Greater London

The questionnaire

Items marked "*" appear on the Welsh version only.

INTERVIEWER: PLEASE CODE AREA WHERE YOU ARE WORKING.

01: Wales
02: Rest of the country

(Route: if coded 01 ask Q.A. Others go to Q.1)

Q.A   For the next series of questions you have the opportunity of answering them in Welsh. The questions are on learning and education. If you would like to answer the questions in Welsh I will be happy to arrange for a Welsh-speaking interviewer to come and interview you at a time that is convenient. Would you like to answer the questions in Welsh, would you prefer to answer the questions in Welsh but would be prepared to answer them in English, or would you carry on answering in English?
01: Would like to answer questions in Welsh
02: Prefer Welsh but will answer in English
03: Will answer in English

(Route: if coded 01 go to Q.B. Others go to Q.1)

Q.B   Will it be okay, therefore, for a Welsh speaking interviewer to give you a call in the next couple of weeks to arrange for the interview to be carried out in Welsh?
01: Yes – acceptable
02: No – not acceptable

SHOW SCREEN

Q.1   Apart from television and radio, what are your main leisure time activities and interests?
01: Arts: painting, pottery, writing, photography etc.
02: Committee work\voluntary service
03: Gardening
04: Going to church\temple\mosque
05: DIY\handicrafts\woodwork
06: Indoor games including chess, bridge
07: Listening to music
08: Music as a performer
09: Physical activities and sports, including walking and keep fit
10: Reading
11: Sewing\knitting\making clothes\embroidery
12: Social activities (family, friends, disco, eating out, pub)
13: Other (please specify)
(N)
(DK)

SHOW SCREEN

Q.2   How often do you do any of the following?
       ...   Visit a public library
       ...   Go to the cinema
       ...   Go to the theatre
       ...   Go to a concert\opera\ballet
       ...   Go to a museum
       ...   Go to an art gallery
       ...   Go to a community centre\social club
       ...   Go to a place of worship

       01:    Once a week or more often
       02:    Less than once a week to once a month
       03:    Less often\never
       (DK)

       I would now like to talk about the sort of learning that people do. Learning can mean practising,
       studying, or reading about something. It can also mean being taught, instructed or coached. This
       is so you can develop skills, knowledge, abilities or understanding of something. Learning can
       also be called education or training. You can do it regularly (each day or month) or you can do it
       for a short period of time. It can be full-time or part-time, done at home, at work, or in another
       place like college. Learning does not have to lead to a qualification. I am interested in any
       learning you have done, whether or not it was finished.

SHOW SCREEN

Q.3   Which of the following statements most applies to you?

       01:    I am currently doing some learning activity now.
       02:    I have done some learning activity in the last 3 years
       03:    I have studied\learnt but it was over 3 years ago
       04:    I have not studied\learnt since I left full time education
       (DK)

(Route: If coded 01 or 02 at Q.3 go to Q.4a, others go to Q.16a)

Q.4a   What subjects are you learning about or have you most recently learnt about?
       PROBE: anything else?
       01:    Accountancy
       02:    Arts: including painting\pottery\sculpture\design
       03:    Basic maths\numeracy
       04:    Basic skills: reading\writing\literacy
       05:    Building trades
       06:    Business studies\administration\management (including HR and marketing)
       07:    Car maintenance
       08:    Carpentry\DIY\Handicrafts
       09:    Communication skills including customer care
       10:    Computer skills\information technology\using the Internet
       11:    Cookery\catering
       12:    Dance
       13:    Dressmaking\tailoring\needlecraft
       14:    Driving (including HGV)
       15:    Engineering (electronic\mechanical\construction)
       16:    English as a second or additional language

17:   English language\literature
18:   Foreign languages (excluding Welsh)
19:   Gardening\horticulture\garden design\floristry
20:   Health and medicine: including nursing and first aid
21:   History\local history
22:   Law\bar exams
23:   Music
24:   Photography
25:   Religion\bible studies\theology
26:   Self development\assertiveness training
27:   Science\maths\statistics
28:   Shorthand\typing\office training
29:   Social sciences\psychology\sociology etc.
30:   Social work\social services\community care
31:   Sports\gymnastics\keep fit
32:   Welsh language
33:   Mother tongue, other than English or Welsh
34:   Other informal\community learning (including learning to learn) (type in)
35:   Other professional and vocational qualifications (type in)
36:   Other academic subjects (type in)
37:   Other 'leisure' subjects (type in)
(DK)

(Route: if more than one subject coded at Q.4a go to Q.4b. Others go to Q.5)

Q.4b   What is the main subject you are learning about or have most recently learnt about?
       (List of answers given at Q.4a)

Q.5   How did you find out about (INSERT SUBJECT)?
       PROBE: Any other ways?
       01:   Friends\family
       02:   Work mates\colleagues
       03:   Printed publicity (posters\leaflets etc) delivered to home
       04:   Printed publicity (posters\leaflets etc) elsewhere
       05:   Newspapers\magazines
       *29: Papur Bro
       06:   College: further education, tertiary, 6th form college
       07:   Adult education centre\evening institute\Workers' Educational Association
       08:   University\higher education institution\Open University
       09:   Community centre\voluntary organisation\religious group
       10:   School
       11:   Trade union\professional association
       12:   Public library
       13:   LSC (Learning and Skills Council), TEC (Training and Enterprise Council)\LEC ELWa
             (Education and Learning Wales)
       14:   SBS (Small Business Service), Chamber of Commerce, Business Connect, Scottish
             Enterprise
       15:   Work: my employer\training officer\personnel officer
       16:   Careers service\advice and guidance service\Connexions\Careers Wales
       17:   Job centre\Job club\UBO\employment service e.g. New Deal
       18:   Town hall\council offices
       19:   learndirect (including the University for Industry (UfI))
       20:   Other telephone helpline, including BBC
       21:   CAB (Citizen's Advice Bureau)\advice centre
       22:   Radio
       *30: Radio – Welsh medium

23: Television
*31: Television – Welsh medium
24: Internet\world wide web\online
25: GP\health centre\clinic
26: Health club\fitness club\leisure club\sports centre
27: Social worker\community outreach worker
28: Other (please specify)
(DK)

SHOW SCREEN

Q.6   On this screen there are some reasons people have given for why they choose to learn about a certain subject or skill. Thinking of your learning of (INSERT SUBJECT), which of the following best describe the reason you started this learning?
(Order of list randomised but 01 and 02 fixed in that order, and 16-19 fixed at bottom)
01: To get a job
02: To get a job with a different employer
03: To change the type of work I do
04: To get a recognised qualification
05: To help in my current job
06: To get a promotion
07: To get a rise in earnings
08: To make my work more satisfying
09: To help me get onto a future course of learning
10: To develop myself as a person
11: To improve my self-confidence
12: I enjoy learning\it gives me pleasure
13: I am interested in the subject\personal interest
14: To meet people
15: As a result of participating in another activity
16: Not really my choice – employer requirement
17: Not really my choice – professional requirement
18: Not really my choice – benefit requirement
19: Only type of learning available
(DK)

SHOW SCREEN

Q.7   Where is the main location that you do or did this learning?
01: Where I work
02: Employer's training centre
03: Other private training centre\conference centre\hotel
04: Job centre\job club\skill centre
05: Local ICT learning centre (e.g. learndirect\UKonline)
06: Adult education centre\evening institute\Workers' Educational Association class
07: Further education college\tertiary\6th form college
08: University\higher education institution\Open University
09: Local primary school
10: Local secondary school
11: Other educational institution
12: Public library
13: Community centre\leisure centre
14: With an informal group e.g. women's group, church etc.
15: Voluntary organisation e.g. pre-school learning alliance, U3A etc
16: Health\fitness\leisure centre\club

17:   While driving\travelling
18:   At home – structured correspondence course or open learning
19:   At home – informal learning\from a book
20:   At home – from radio\TV
21:   At home – using a computer, CD Rom, Internet
22:   Other (please specify)
(DK)

SHOW SCREEN

Q.8   How easy is it to get to where your learning takes or took place?
01:   Don't or didn't have to travel: learn(t) at home\work
02:   Very easy
03:   Fairly easy
04:   Fairly difficult
05:   Very difficult
(DK)

Q.9   Thinking about (INSERT SUBJECT), about how many hours a week do you or did you spend on learning?

SHOW SCREEN

Q.10   Thinking about (INSERT SUBJECT), how long do you expect to, or did you study for this altogether?
01:   Less than 1 week
02:   1 week – 1 month
03:   Over 1 month – 3 months
04:   Over 3 months – 6 months
05:   7 – 12 months
06:   Over 1 – 2 years
07:   Over 2 years
(DK)

SHOW SCREEN

Q.11a   What qualifications, if any, are (were if coded 02 at Q.3) you aiming towards?
01:   None\not aiming for qualification
02:   GCSE grades A*-C\SCE Credit Level Standard Grades
03:   GCSE grades D-G\SCE Foundation Level Standard Grades
04:   A level, A\S level, S level\AVCE\Scottish Highers
20:   RSA
21:   City and Guilds
16:   Open College Network (OCN) Credit
22:   BTEC\SCOTVEC\SCOTEV
05:   Diploma in Higher Education (DipHE)
06:   Foundation Degree
07:   Degree (BA, BSc, BEd)
08:   Higher degree (e.g. MA, MSc, PhD)
09:   Nursing\medical\clinical qualification
10:   PGCE or other teaching qualification
11:   Modern Apprenticeship
12:   NVQ\SVQ
13:   GNVQ\GSVQ
14:   ONC\OND

15:   HNC\HND
17:   Other post-graduate qualification (please specify)
18:   Other professional qualification (please specify)
19:   Other qualifications (please specify)
(DK)

(Route: if coded 02 or 03 at Q.11a ask Q.11b. Others see Q.11c)

Q.11b   How many GCSEs or SCEs are (were if coded 02 at Q.3) you aiming for?
        (Type in box, allow 2 digits)
        (DK)

(Route: if coded 20 at Q.11a ask Q.11c. Others see Q.11d)

SHOW SCREEN

Q.11c   What is (was if coded 02 at Q.3) the level of RSA you are (were if coded 02 at Q.3) aiming for?
        01:   Higher Diploma
        02:   Advanced Diploma or Certificate
        03:   First Diploma
        04:   Certificate
        05:   Other RSA qualification (please specify)
        (DK)

(Route: if coded 04 at Q.11a ask Q.11d. Others see Q.11e)

SHOW SCREEN

Q.11d   How many A, A\S, S levels, AVCEs or Scottish Highers are (were if coded 02 at Q.3) you aiming for?
        01:   -1-
        02:   -2-
        03:   -3-
        04:    4 or more
        (DK)

(Route: if coded 12 at Q.11a ask Q.11e. Others see Q.11f)

SHOW SCREEN

Q.11e   What is (was if coded 02 at Q.3) the level of NVQ\SVQ you are (were if coded 02 at Q.3) aiming for?
        01:   Level 5
        02:   Level 4
        03:   Level 3
        04:   Level 2
        05:   Level 1
        06:   Units towards NVQ\SVQ
        07:   Other NVQ (specify)
        (DK)

(Route: if coded 13 at Q.11a ask Q.11f. Others see Q.11g)

SHOW SCREEN

Q.11f   What is (was if coded 02 at Q.3) the level of GNVQ\GSVQ you are (were if coded 02 at Q.3)
        aiming for?
        01:   Advanced
        02:   Intermediate
        03:   Foundation
        04:   Other GNVQ\QSVQ qualification (specify)
        (DK)

(Route: if coded 16 at Q.11a ask Q.11g. Others see Q.11h)

SHOW SCREEN

Q.11g   What is (was if coded 02 at Q.3) the level of OCN credit you are (were if coded 02 at Q.3) aiming
        for?
        02:   Level 3
        03:   Level 2
        04:   Level 1
        06:   Entry level
        05:   Other OCN qualification (specify)
        (DK)

(Route: if coded 21 at Q.11a ask Q.11h. Others see Q.11i)

SHOW SCREEN

Q.11h   What is (was if coded 02 at Q.3) the level of City and Guilds you are (were if coded 02 at Q.3)
        aiming for?
        01:   Part 3\Final\Advanced Craft
        02:   Part 2\Craft\Intermediate
        03:   Part 1
        04:   Other City and Guilds qualification (please specify)
        (DK)

(Route: if coded 22 at Q.11a ask Q.11i. Others go to Q.12)

SHOW SCREEN

Q.11i   What is (was if coded 02 at Q.3) the level of BTEC\SCOTVEC\SCOTEV you are (were if coded 02
        at Q.3) aiming for?
        01:   Higher Certificate Diploma
        02:   National Certificate Diploma
        03:   First\General Diploma
        04:   First\General Certificate
        05:   Other BTEC\SCOTVEC\SCOTEV qualification (please specify)
        (DK)

SHOW SCREEN

Q.12   Did you complete your learning or course?
        01:   Yes, completed it
        02:   No, gave up before end
        03:   Still studying it
        (DK)

SHOW SCREEN

Q.13   Can you identify any changes or benefits that have happened as a result of your learning?

(Scripter: randomise order of list but fix 01 and 02 in that order)
01:    I have got\expect to get a job
02:    I have got\expect to get a job with a different employer
03:    I have changed\expect to change the type of work I do
04:    I have got\expect to get a recognised qualification
05:    I have been helped\expect to be helped in my current job
06:    I have got\expect to get a promotion or a rise in earnings
07:    My work has become\I expect my work to become more satisfying
08:    I have moved\expect to move onto a further course of learning
09:    I have developed myself as a person
10:    My self-confidence has improved
11:    I have met new people\made new friends
12:    My health has improved
13:    I enjoy learning more: more aware of the benefits of learning, know I can learn etc.
14:    My children\my family have become more interested in learning
15:    I am more involved in local events and issues
(DK)

SHOW SCREEN

Q.14   Who pays or paid the fees for this learning?
PROBE: Who else?
01:    No fees to pay
02:    Myself
03:    Family\relative
04:    My employer\potential employer paid outside fees
05:    My employer funded provision of learning
06:    Government training scheme e.g. New Deal
07:    ILA (Individual Learning Account)
08:    Help from my institution e.g. access funds, bursaries etc.
08:    Local authority grant
09:    Other government funding
10:    Charitable trust or other non-government organisation
11:    Other (specify)
(DK)

SHOW SCREEN

Q.15   Sometimes learning can have other costs apart from fees. The following are some of the costs that people can experience when they do some learning. Thinking about your main learning of (INSERT SUBJECT), has it led or did it lead to any costs like these?
01:    No other costs
02:    Loss of wages\salary\overtime
03:    Loss of benefit(s)
04:    Cost of childcare
05:    Travel costs
06:    Costs of equipment (e.g. books\computers\Internet charges)
07:    Other (specify)
(DK)

SHOW SCREEN

Q.16a   What is the highest level of examination or qualification that you now hold, including any that
        you may have gained since leaving full-time education?
        01:   No qualifications held
        02:   O level\CSE 1\Matriculation\School Certificate
        03:   GCSE grade A*-C\SCE Credit Level Standard Grade
        04:   GCSE grade D-G\SCE Foundation Level Standard Grade
        05:   A level, A\S level, S level, AVCE, Scottish Higher
        22:   RSA\Pitman's
        23:   City and Guilds
        18:   Open College Network (OCN) Credit
        24:   BTEC\SCOTVEC\SCOTEV
        06:   Diploma in Higher Education (DipHE)
        07:   Foundation Degree
        08:   Degree (BA, BSc, BEd)
        09:   Higher Degree (MA, MSc, PhD)
        11:   Nursing\medical\clinical qualification
        12:   PGCE or other teaching qualification
        13:   Apprenticeship\Modern Apprenticeship
        14:   NVQ\SVQ
        15:   GNVQ\GSVQ
        16:   ONC\OND
        17:   HNC\HND
        19:   Other post-graduate qualification (specify)
        20:   Other professional qualification (specify)
        21:   Other qualifications (please specify)
        (DK)

(Route: if coded 02 at Q.16a ask Q.16aa. Others see Q.16b)

SHOW SCREEN

Q.16aa How many subjects at O level\CSE grade 1\Matriculation\School Certificate do you hold?
        (Type in box, allow 2 digits)
        (DK)

(Route: if coded 03 at Q.16a ask Q.16b. Others see Q.16c)

SHOW SCREEN

Q.16b   How many GCSE's grades A* to C, or SCE Credit Level Standard Grades, do you hold?
        01:   -1-
        02:   -2-
        03:   -3-
        04:   -4-
        05:   5 or more (type in)
        (DK)

(Route: if coded 04 at Q.16a ask Q.16c. Others see Q.16d)

SHOW SCREEN

Q.16c How many GCSE's grades D to G, or SCE Foundation Level Standard Grades, do you hold?
      01: -1-
      02: -2-
      03: -3-
      04: -4-
      05: 5 or more (type in)
      (DK)

(Route: if coded 05 at Q.16a ask Q.16d. Others see Q.16e)

SHOW SCREEN

Q.16d How many A levels, A\S levels, S levels, AVCEs, or Scottish Highers do you hold?
      01: -1-
      02: -2-
      03: -3-
      04: 4 or more
      (DK)

(Route: if coded 14 at Q.16a ask Q.16e. Others go to Q.16f)

SHOW SCREEN

Q.16e What is the highest level of NVQ\SVQ you hold?
      01: Level 5
      02: Level 4
      03: Level 3
      04: Level 2
      05: Level 1
      06: Units towards NVQ\SVQ
      07: Other NVQ (specify)
      (DK)

(Route: if coded 15 at Q.16a ask Q.16f. Others see Q.16g)

SHOW SCREEN

Q.16f What is the highest level of GNVQ\GSVQ you hold?
      01: Advanced
      02: Intermediate
      03: Foundation
      04: Other GNVQ\QSVQ qualification (specify)
      (DK)

(Route: if coded 18 at Q.16a ask Q.16g. Others see Q.16h)

SHOW SCREEN

Q.16g What is the highest level of OCN you hold?
      02: Level 3
      03: Level 2
      04: Level 1
      06: Entry level
      05: Other OCN qualification (specify)
      (DK)

(Route: if coded 22 at Q.16a ask Q.16h. Others see Q.16i)

SHOW SCREEN

Q.16h   What is the highest level of RSA\Pitman's you hold?
         01:   Higher Diploma
         02:   Advanced Diploma or Certificate
         03:   First Diploma
         04:   Certificate
         05:   Other RSA\Pitman's qualification (please specify)
         (DK)

(Route: if coded 23 at Q.16a ask Q.16i. Others see Q.16j)

SHOW SCREEN

Q.16i   What is the highest level of City and Guilds you hold?
         01:   Part 3\Final\Advanced Craft
         02:   Part 2\Craft\Intermediate
         03:   Part 1
         04:   Other City and Guilds qualification (please specify)
         (DK)

(Route: if coded 24 at Q.16a ask Q.16j. Others go to Q.17)

SHOW SCREEN

Q.16j   What is the highest level of BTEC\SCOTVEC\SCOTEV you hold?
         01:   Higher Certificate Diploma
         02:   National Certificate Diploma
         03:   First\General Diploma
         04:   First\General Certificate
         05:   Other BTEC\SCOTVEC\SCOTEV qualification (please specify)
         (DK)

SHOW SCREEN

Q.17   How old were you when you finished full-time education?
         01:   14 or under
         02:   15
         03:   16
         04:   17
         05:   18
         06:   19
         07:   20
         08:   21
         09:   22
         10:   23
         11:   24
         12:   25 or more
         13:   Still a full-time student: school\college\university
         (DK)

SHOW SCREEN

Q.18   How likely are you to take up any learning in the next 3 years?
      01:   Very likely
      02:   Fairly likely
      03:   Fairly unlikely
      04:   Very unlikely
      (DK)

(Route: if coded 02 to 04 or DK at Q.18 go to Q.19. Others go to Q.20)

SHOW SCREEN

Q.19   From the following list what, if anything, would you say are the main things preventing you from learning these days?
      PROBE: Anything else?
      01:   Not interested\don't want to
      02:   Cost\money\can't afford it
      03:   Childcare arrangements\caring for others
      04:   Transport\too far to travel
      05:   Work\other time pressures
      06:   I don't like being in groups of people I don't know
      07:   I don't know what is available
      08:   I feel I am too old
      09:   I am too ill\too disabled
      10:   I am worried about being out alone
      11:   I haven't got round to doing it
      12:   I feel no need to learn anymore
      13:   I don't feel colleges\centres are welcoming
      14:   I do not have the qualifications I need
      15:   I do not have the abilities I need
      16:   I am put off by tests and exams
      17:   I am too nervous about the idea of starting learning
      18:   I don't feel confident enough
      19:   I would not be able to get time off work
      20:   I've tried learning in the past and it has been unsuccessful
      21:   No suitable courses are available
  * 24:   Lack of opportunity to learn in Welsh
  * 25:   Lack of opportunity to learn in other mother tongue
      22:   Lack of opportunity to learn in other tongue
      23:   Other (please specify)
      (N)
      (DK)

Q.20   What (else), if anything, would you be most interested in learning about if you could?
      (List as Q.4a)

SHOW SCREEN

Q.21   I will now read out a list of statements people have made about different types of learning. For each one, please tell me how much you agree or disagree. So firstly, how much do you agree or disagree with

   ...   Learning is enjoyable for its own sake

   ...   I am confident about learning new skills

   ...   People who get training find their jobs are more interesting

   ...   People who get trained at work end up with better promotion or better pay

   ...   People should not be expected to learn new skills for their career in their own time

   ...   There is not enough help and advice available about the different sorts of learning people can do

   ...   I don't see why I should pay for learning that is to do with my job or career

     01: Agree strongly
     02: Agree
     03: Neither agree nor disagree
     04: Disagree
     05: Disagree strongly
     (DK)

SHOW SCREEN

Q.22   I will now read two more statements and, again, for each one, please tell me how much you agree or disagree. So firstly, how much do you agree or disagree with

   ...   In general most people can be trusted

   ...   I am optimistic about my future

     01: Agree strongly
     02: Agree
     03: Neither agree nor disagree
     04: Disagree
     05: Disagree strongly
     (DK)

SHOW SCREEN

Q.23   Which of the following statements, if any, applies to your recent or current situation?

     01: I have started a family
     02: I have lost my job\ been made redundant
     03: I have started a new job\been promoted
     04: I have taken early retirement\retired
     05: I have been involved in a broken marriage\broken up with my partner
     06: I have recently lost a partner\spouse
     07: I have moved home\moved to a new area
     08: I wanted\want promotion at work
     09: I wanted\want to help my children learn
     10: I had a serious illness
     11: I have a new\increasing disability
     (N)
     (DK)

SHOW SCREEN

Q.24   Which, if any, of these had any bearing on your decision to take up learning?
       (List as at Q.23 filtered on answers at Q.23)

Q.25   Have you heard of the European Social Fund?
        PROBE: You may have heard of it as ESF?
        01:   Yes
        02:   No
        (DK)

(Route: if coded 01 at Q.25 ask Q.26. Others go to Q.27a)

Q.26   What do you think the European Social Fund does?
        PROBE: What else? PROBE: Anything else?

        (Open-ended)

SHOW SCREEN

Q.27a   Which of these do you have regular access to?
        PROBE: Any others?
        01:   Mobile phone
        02:   CD player
        03:   DVD player
        04:   Computer\PC\laptop
        05:   Internet via normal phone line
        06:   Internet via Broadband connection
        (N)
        (DK)

(Route: if 05 or 06 coded, go to Q.27b. Others go to Q.28)

SHOW SCREEN

Q.27b   Which of these activities have you ever used the Internet for?
        PROBE: Any others?
        01:   Using e-mail
        02:   Using chat rooms or sites
        03:   Finding information about goods and services (including holidays, flights, houses, etc.)
        04:   Buying or ordering tickets, goods or services (excluding shares and financial services)
        05:   Personal banking, financial and investment activities
        06:   Looking for jobs or work
        07:   Downloading software, including games
        08:   Playing or downloading music
        09:   Finding information related to children's schoolwork
        10:   Finding information for my learning\training
        11:   Learning on\off-line
        12:   Using or accessing government or official services
        13:   General browsing or surfing
        14:   Other things
        (N)
        (DK)

SHOW SCREEN

Q.27c And which of these activities do you mostly use the Internet for?
    01: Using e-mail
    02: Using chat rooms or sites
    03: Finding information about goods and services (including holidays,
         flights, houses, etc.)
    04: Buying or ordering tickets, goods or services (excluding shares and financial services)
    05: Personal banking, financial and investment activities
    06: Looking for jobs or work
    07: Downloading software, including games
    08: Playing or downloading music
    09: Finding information related to children's schoolwork
    10: Finding information for my learning\training
    11: Learning on\off-line
    12: Using or accessing government or official services
    13: General browsing or surfing
    14: Other things
    (N)
    (DK)

SHOW SCREEN

Q.28 People of different cultural backgrounds may have different needs in relation to studying and
    learning. With this in mind, can you tell me which of the following best describes you?
    01: White
    02: Black – Caribbean
    03: Black – African
    04: Black – British
    05: Black – other (please specify)
    06: Bangladeshi
    07: Indian
    08: Pakistani
    09: Chinese
    10: Asian – British
    11: Asian – other (specify)
    12: Arab
    13: Cypriot
    14: Other (specify)
    (R)

SHOW SCREEN

Q.29 What is your mother tongue, that is the language you first learned as a child?
    01: Arabic
    02: Bengali
    03: English
    04: Greek
    05: Gujarati
    06: Hindi
    07: Punjabi
    08: Somali
    13: Turkish
    09: Urdu
    10: Yemeni

11:   Welsh
12:   Other (specify)
(DK)

SHOW SCREEN

Q.30   Through which language do you prefer to learn?
01:   Arabic
02:   Bengali
03:   English
04:   Greek
05:   Gujarati
06:   Hindi
07:   Punjabi
08:   Somali
13:   Turkish
09:   Urdu
10:   Yemeni
11:   Welsh
12:   Other (specify)
(DK)

References

ACACE (1982a) *Adults: their educational experience and needs*, Leicester, ACACE

ACACE (1982b) *Continuing education: from policies to practice*, Leicester, ACACE

Aldridge, F. (2001) *Fees Survey 2000-2001: Indicators of fee levels charges to part-time adult students by Local Education Authorities and Colleges*, Leicester, NIACE

Aldridge, F. and Tuckett, A (2002) *Two steps forward, one step back: The NIACE survey on adult participation in learning 2002*, Leicester, NIACE

Beinart, S. and Smith, P. (1998) *National Adult Learning Survey 1997*, Sheffield, DfES

Cross, K.P. (1981) *Adults as Learners*, San-Francisco, Jossey-Bass

DfEE (1998) *The Learning Age: a renaissance for a new Britain*, London, The Stationery Office

DfEE (2001) *Skills for life: the national strategy for improving adult literacy and numeracy skills*, Nottingham, DfEE

DfES (2001) *Schools – achieving success* (White Paper), Nottingham, DfES

La Valle, I and Blake, M. (2001) National Adult Learning Survey 2002 (TT321), Nottingham, DfES

Payne, J. (2001) *Rural learning: A practical guide to developing learning opportunities in the countryside*, Leicester, NIACE

Russell, N. and Drew, N. (2001) *ICT Access and Use* (DfEE Research Brief 252), RSGB

Sargant, N. and Aldridge, F. (forthcoming) *Adult Learning and Social Division: a persistent pattern Volume 2* Issues arising from the 2002 NIACE adult participation in learning survey, Leicester, NIACE

Sargant, N. (1991) *Learning and 'Leisure': a study of adult participation in learning and its policy implications*, Leicester, NIACE

Sargant, N. (1993) *Learning for a Purpose*, Leicester, NIACE

Sargant, N. (2000a) *Motivation for and barriers to participation in adult learning – a study across Norway, Spain and Great Britain* (MOBA), Leicester, NIACE

Sargant, N. (2000b) *The Learning Divide Revisited: a report on the findings of a UK-wide survey on adult participation in education and learning*, Leicester, NIACE

Sargant, N. with Field, J., Francis, H., Schuller, T. and Tuckett, A. (1997) *The Learning Divide: a study of participation in adult learning in the United Kingdom*, Leicester, NIACE

Schuller, T., Brasset Grundy, A., Green, A., Hammond, C. and Preston, J. (2002) *Learning, Continuity and Change in Adult Life*, London, Centre for Research on the Wider Benefits of Learning (RR3)

SCPR (1997) *National Adult Learning Survey*, Sheffield, DfEE

Skaalvik, E.M. and Finbak, L. (2001) *Adult Education in Great Britain, Norway and Spain: a comparative study of participation, motivation and barriers*, Trondheim, The Norwegian Institute for Adult Education

Tough, A. (1971) *The Adult's Learning Projects: A fresh approach to theory and practice in adult learning*, Toronto, Ontario Institute for Studies in Education

Tyers, C. and Aston, J (2002) *What difference did it make? Impact of the Adult and Community Learning Fund*, London, IES